MACHINE BEAUTY

The MasterMinds series:

These concise and accessible books present cutting-edge ideas by leading thinkers in a highly readable format, each title a crystallization of a lifetime's work and thought.

Other books in the MasterMinds series include:

Finding Flow by MIHALY CSIKSZENTMIHALYI

After God: The Future of Religion by DON CUPITT

Extraordinary Minds by HOWARD GARDNER

Future contributors include:

STEWART BRAND

JOHN MADDOX

JOHN SEARLE

SHERRY TURKLE

Praise for BasicBooks' Science Masters series:

"This is good publishing. PBS, eat your heart out."
—Kirkus Reviews

"Aimed at busy, nonmathematical readers, this precise series evinces solid quality control and begins under highly favorable auspices."
—A. L. A. Booklist

"If this standard is maintained, the Science Masters series looks set to play a major role in the responsible popularization of sciences."
—New Scientist

MACHINE BEAUTY

ELEGANCE AND THE HEART OF TECHNOLOGY

DAVID GELERNTER

MasterMinds

BasicBooks
A Subsidiary of Perseus Books, L.L.C.

The Master Minds Series is a global publishing venture consisting of original books written by leading thinkers and published by a worldwide team of publishers assembled by John Brockman. The series was conceived by Anthony Cheetham of Orion Publishing and John Brockman of Brockman Inc., a New York literary agency, and developed in coordination with BasicBooks.

The Master Minds name and marks are owned and licensed to the publisher by Brockman Inc.

Published by BasicBooks,
A Subsidiary of Perseus Books, L.L.C.

Designed by Elliott Beard

Library of Congress Cataloging-in-Publication Data

Gelernter, David Hillel.
    Machine beauty : elegance and the heart of
technology / David Gelernter. — 1st ed.
        p.   cm. — (MasterMinds)
    Includes index.
    ISBN 0-465-04516-2
    1. Human-computer interaction.   2. Computer
software—Human factors.   3. Computers—Design
and construction.   I. Title. II. Series.
QA76.9.H85G46   1997
004'.01—dc21   97-14613
                                                           CIP

98 99 00 01 02 ❖/RRD 10 9 8 7 6 5 4 3 2 1

⇥ACKNOWLEDGMENTS

I have drawn for this book on many sources, but three were especially important: Steven Levy's *Insanely Great*, Howard Rheingold's *Tools for Thought*, and David Billington's work in general. My colleagues in computer science have provided me with a wisdom of all sorts over the years; advice from Ben Shneiderman and Alan Kay was particularly useful on the *Machine Beauty* project. This book owes a lot to my students and colleagues at Yale, particularly Martin Schultz, who made the Yale Computer Science Department as fine a place to ponder computing as any in the country; Eric Freeman's dissertation research was especially important to the discussion in chapter 5. Basic Books is an impressive operation—I am particularly grateful to John Donatich for his help and perseverance. And finally, three long-suffering people without whom I would never accomplish a damned thing: Chris Hatchell, my colleague Nicholas Carriero, and my wife, Jane. I don't understand why they do it, but they made the book (and a lot of other things) possible.

Deep Beauty

The sense of beauty is a tuning fork in the brain that hums when we stumble on something beautiful. We enjoy the resonant hum and seek it out. And when we return numb and weary from a round of shoveling the grim gray snow of life, beauty is the hearth, beauty's the fire, beauty's the cup of coffee (the fragrance, the saucer's clink, the curl of cream) that makes the whole business seem almost worthwhile. Ponder long enough as you sip and life can turn inside out under your gaze like a trick profile, and coffee and hearth become the reason snow exists, and beauty explains the world. Strangely enough, beauty is also a truth-and-rightness meter, and science and technology could not exist without it. Its tuning-fork hum guides scientists toward truth and technologists toward stronger and more useful machines. It leads the way forward.

This book explains how beauty drives the computer revolution: how lust for beauty and elegance underpinned the most important discoveries in computational history and continues to push research onward today. Why computer scientists are like the craftsman-engineer Henri Vaillancourt, who, as he carries out a long series of intricate maneuvers in the process of building a birch bark canoe just as the Indians did, drawing on deep knowledge of trees, tools, woodworking, canoe architecture, and canoe dynamics, is guided by a single criterion—a criterion that, according to reporter-author John McPhee, "is always the same: 'it looks good.'" The best computer scientists are, like Vaillancourt, technologists who crave beauty.

There is the ever-present danger when you discuss beauty in science, mathematics, and technology that readers will assume the word is being used metaphorically. People will react to such discussions the way they might to the news that some rich and famous playboy is feeling mopey. Just how unhappy could Crown Prince Fluvial be? Considering that he owns a dozen yachts, dominates international chess and beach volleyball competition, and has to fight off beautiful women with a broom? We figure that if he is "unhappy," it could only be in a relative or metaphorical sense. And could a mathematical proof, scientific theory, or piece of software be "beautiful" in the real, literal way that a painting or symphony or rose can be beautiful?

Yes.

The beauty of a proof or machine lies in a happy marriage of simplicity and power—*power* meaning the ability to accomplish a wide range of tasks, get a lot done. The power and simplicity criterion applies to birch bark canoes, suspension bridges, programming languages, scientific theories, and machines of all kinds. I call this type of beauty "machine beauty"; there is always a happy couple (power married to simplicity) at the heart of it. Not every marriage is happy. Bringing power and simplicity to bear doesn't guarantee machine beauty—just makes it possible, and nothing else does.

Machine beauty is unlike a painting's beauty in some ways. Motion usually has something to do with it—actual motion for mechanical machines, logical motion for a proof or theory. (Of course, logical motion is part of musical or narrative beauty also.) The more abstract types of machine beauty (what you find in mathematics, for example) require considerable knowledge in order to grasp. (Knowledge can intensify an artwork's beauty also, but even the most austere of Bach fugues has a sensual appeal that can reach out and grab any child in a way mathematics cannot.) But machine beauty *can* have as much immediate, sensual appeal as any other kind. By no means is it always austere or hard to grasp. "There is no country in the world," Oscar Wilde wrote in the late nineteenth century, "where machinery is so beautiful as in America. I have always wished to believe that the line of strength and the line of beauty are one. That wish was realized when I contemplated American machinery. . . . The rise and fall of the steel rods"—he is now describing the Chicago waterworks—"the symmetrical motion of great wheels is the most beautiful rhythmic thing I have ever seen."

You might experience something resembling machine beauty, even if you are no scientist or engineer, when you drive a nail into a board with one clean, graceful hammer stroke; you feel the beauty of ease and power mated, machine beauty, beautiful functioning. What makes a beautiful catch in baseball? It must be graceful and look easy. It must be powerful, too—must accomplish something significant. If I make a casual toss, you cannot make a beautiful catch. If you are watching average bullfighters, Hemingway wrote, "whatever extraordinary things they do will look difficult rather than easy." Beauty requires power and ease. "If the dance is right," Fred Astaire said, "there shouldn't be a single superfluous movement." Power and simplicity mated. "Vigorous writing is concise," William Strunk wrote; "a sentence should contain no unnecessary words, a paragraph no unnecessary sentences, for the same reason that a drawing should have no unnecessary lines and a machine no unnecessary parts." "The attraction of these new American forms," writes the art historian C. Edison Armi about the 1950s show cars that paved the way for the extraordinary designs of the early '60s, "was not just their brutish strength but their simplicity." Power married to simplicity equals machine beauty. This beauty equation is the most fundamental in science and technology; it underlies all the others.

Why does the equation hold? That is a question for physiologists and psychologists; for our purposes, it just does. Why do roses smell sweet and trash dumps not? Because human beings are built that way. In any case, had an omnipotent creator set out to equip man with a truth-seeking physiology, He could hardly have done better than to provide us with this peculiar beauty sense of ours.

Many different sorts of beauty are part of this story, ranging from the austere elegance of powerful mathematics to the beautiful lines of a bridge or locomotive or a picture on a computer screen. The beauty of a bridge or computer-screen picture bears an obvious family relationship to a painting's or sculpture's—and a beautiful "technology object" might reflect the hard work of an art school–trained designer who hasn't the slightest doubt that he is doing art; tell him otherwise and he will set you straight fast. Mathematical beauty has a different flavor, and arises with no help from designers. But the austere, nonvisual beauty of mathematics is one end of a spectrum leading to bridges and, past bridges, to everyday technology objects: toasters, telephones, the images on computer screens.

The writer and structural engineer David Billington describes the Swiss engineer Robert Maillart's celebrated Salginatobel bridge of 1930:

> An object of mystery and wonder. . . . Arising in a setting of almost primitive mountain simplicity, the bridge almost immediately became an important force in the most so-

phisticated circles of avant-garde intellectuals. Considered now to be a work of art, the design was originally chosen because it was the least expensive proposal.

Bridges put engineering and mathematics into physical form. The structural engineer makes choices within a tightly constrained aesthetic world; he wants his structure to be cheap and to stand up. He may yearn for the special piquancy of a bridge made out of carved alabaster or translucent fuschia rice paper or marigolds, but that's just too bad. The constraints he is under do not, however, eliminate the aesthetic side of the task; they only make it harder, just as it is harder to write a strict four-part fugue than a cowboy song. Inside the cramped closet of permissible choices, the great bridge builder searches aggressively for the beautiful solution. Distinguished structural engineers are the farthest thing from aesthetic naifs. "Beginning with Telford's 1812 essay on bridges," Billington writes, successful structural engineers "have been conscious of, and have written about, the aesthetic ideals that guided their work."

The intellectual beauty of mathematics and engineering and the visual beauty of fine bridges are closely linked. The great physicist Richard Feynman describes Hoover Dam: as you descend from the top, the dam's thickness widens in a beautiful curve that reflects the increasing water pressure as you go deeper. "If some future archeologist" were to uncover the dam, Feynman writes, he would be bound to admire this beautiful curve; "but also the explorers from some great future civilization will look at the generators and transformers and say: 'Notice that every iron piece has a beautifully efficient shape.'" Visual beauty and "intellectual," scientific beauty are linked and intertwined in a single monumental structure.

At the opposite end of the machine beauty spectrum, at the farthest point from the austere loveliness of physics and mathematics, you find objects like the great designer Henry

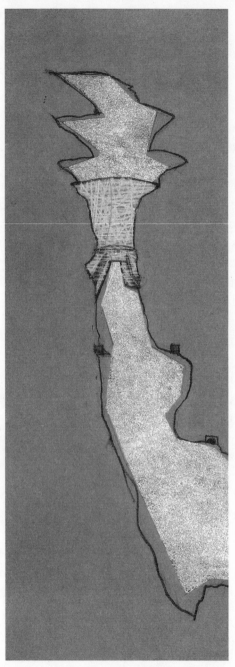

An English visitor wrote in 1936 of Hoover Dam that "it is a symbol of the new man, a new world, a new way of life . . . it is a thing of beauty. . . . The impression it makes on any sensitive observer is not unlike that made by a massive work of art."

Dreyfuss's 1937 telephone. It is not elegant in the way proofs are, or dams; it reflects the work of a designer who was free to draw whatever he wanted, up to a point. Yet the resulting design does not seem arbitrary in the least. Its seeming inevitable rightness is a large part of its greatness. It expresses an underlying technology just as clearly as the dam's shape does.

If you make a dam the wrong shape, it will crumble. If you shape a telephone like a Volkswagen or a tomato, it can still work. Some technologies allow greater design leeway than others. But divining the shape that seems inevitable, creating the "inevitability illusion"—the impression that you are looking at the pure visual embodiment of science or engineering—is an art pure and simple, whether you are designing dams or vacuum cleaners. It takes a gifted structural engineer or designer to make the right choices and create that illusion. When the illusion succeeds, the outcome is technology that works beautifully and *is* beautiful.

The quality of quintessentiality is hard to pin down but

too important to ignore. It is a widely cited standard. "A useful object has a 'natural' form," one designer writes, "which when it is in complete harmony with its function is perceived as having a special 'rightness' or 'fit' that borders on art." Or rather *is* art. The Empire State Building is *the* skyscraper (as Hoover is *the* dam, Dreyfuss's *the* phone); its shape seems less designed than at long last discovered, like a law of physics. It is so right for its purpose that it draws answering echoes from the mind, like *helloooo*ing into a resonant cave—and yet no one ever ordained that a skyscraper needs a broad squat base, squarish shaft, and spire on top. We tend to think of science as discovery, art as invention, but that is not the whole truth, as classical Greeks understood; good scientists and good artists are piano tuners listening attentively, as they finagle, for the sound of exact rightness.

The functional machine beauty of science and engineering married to the plain old static beauty of lovely lines yields "deep beauty," many levels resonating with and reinforcing one another as they do in the Salginatobel bridge or the Hoover Dam or the Dreyfuss telephone. "Whoever understands the dynamics of pitch in propeller blades," wrote Philip Johnson in his introduction to the 1934 *Machine Art* exhibit at New York's Museum of Modern Art,

> or the distribution of forces in a ball bearing so that he can participate imaginatively in the action of mechanical functions is likely to find that this knowledge enhances the beauty of the objects. For most people, the beauty of that ingenious engine, the Gothic vault, is augmented by a knowledge of the mechanics which govern its structure and visible form.

It works the other way, too: "the action of mechanical functions" is a source of beauty in itself, which you appreciate more when it is framed in beautiful lines. Deep beauty, "resonant beauty" in which many types of loveliness reinforce one another, is a principal topic of this book. It is one of civilization's great attainments, but we rarely appreciate or understand or even notice it. Presented with a deep beauty symphony we only hear the second violins. But, after all, understanding big pictures, grasping the ways in which separate parts reinforce one another, is a thing at which our nose-to-the-ground, call-in-the-specialists! civilization is consistently rotten.

This book has two themes twining around each other like a double spiral staircase, meeting at every turn—one positive and one negative.

The first is this: machine beauty is the driving force behind technology and science. It has been crucial to the development of computing; it has been at the core of nearly every major breakthrough in the field; and it is the ultimate guarantee of success with the public. When you step back and take a good look, it is also lovely to contemplate. My first goal is to conduct a quick tour of computing and point out some of the machine beauty highlights. And I will pause on our way in, and again coming out, to glance at machine beauty elsewhere in science and technology.

There is a negative countertheme also: machine beauty bothers us. We act as a society as if our goal were not to nurture or celebrate it but to stamp it out. And our perversity has consequences. We give our scientists and technologists wrong training. We guide our technology enterprises badly. We force some of our most promising new technologies to crawl through bizarre obstacle courses on their bellies instead of greeting them with roses. We tolerate junk cheerfully—in the form of commercial software, for example—that hurts our productivity and adds nuisance to our lives. A "paradox of beauty," in short—we know that machine beauty is crucially important, but it kills us to say so.

Why? That is a hard question and there is no single answer. But at base, machine beauty rubs us wrong. It confuses us, and doesn't seem to fit. We still worship science and technology—although we are rarely honest or clearheaded enough, nowadays, to own up to the fact; and to our minds science is objective, logical, analytic, austere, esoteric, highly specialized, and masculine. That our best scientists and technologists are guided by aesthetics is embarrassing. (Although it is false that love of beauty is a specifically feminine characteristic, we think it is. And to be fair, the average woman *is* more willing than the average man to talk about aesthetic qualities—maybe because she is more apt to notice them in the first place. Maybe not.) Insisting that beauty is at the heart of science and technology is like ordering wine at lunch, or tacking ruffles to your office furniture—it takes a serious proposition and makes it frilly and frivolous.

It ruins, also, the simpleminded classification we have lived by for a long time. We believe implicitly that the scientist is one type, the artist a radically different one. In fact, the scientific and artistic personalities overlap more than they differ, and the higher we shimmy into the leafy canopy of talent, the closer the two enterprises seem. The typical first-year physics text never uses the word *beauty*, but it is no accident that Richard Feynman's text—the work of a great scientist and one of the century's great books—uses it all the time.

Software is hard to grasp, literally and otherwise. Let's start with everyday technology objects.

Some inspired technologists achieve beauty on their own. Some push their designs to a certain point, find them aesthetically wanting, and call in designers to finish the job. (There is no reason, in principle, why a scientist couldn't call in a designer to help finish a theory or formulate an experiment; but the problems tend to be more readily communicated in technology than in science.) The designers of the Gestetner duplicating machine made it work but failed to make it beautiful. So in 1929 Sigmund Gestetner looked up young Raymond Loewy in Manhattan and asked him to redesign the awkward, busy-looking duplicator; and by the way, he was sailing for England in three days, so Loewy had better step on it.

A design emerged right on schedule three days later and remained in production, basically unchanged, for forty years. Loewy's machine was sleek and neat and simple. And it functioned better than the original: worked better as office furniture. The old machine had flared-out legs. They were a hazard; people tripped over them. Loewy straightened them. Obvious change? Certainly, in retrospect. An old photograph shows Gestetner and Loewy side by side as the client inspects the clay model for the first time. Gestetner's smile is unrehearsed—radiant and delighted. The photo is strangely moving.

Loewy's firm designed cars for Studebaker. As usual, aesthetics and function improved simultaneously and were jumbled up in Loewy's thinking: "Weight is the enemy ... whatever saves weight saves cost. The car must look fast, whether in motion or stationary."

It was good work, but Loewy's Gestetner machine is obsolete. Marcel Breuer's 1928 Cesca chair is not, and is likely to remain popular for as long as people sit down. It is a masterwork of bent steel tubing with canvas seat and back—or, in another early version, caned seat and back in wooden frames. Comfortable, elegant, sturdy, of relatively cheap materials— deep beauty, a textbook example.

It looks obvious and inevitable today, but the idea of making residential furniture of steel tubing was new with Breuer; he came up with it in 1925, and there was nothing obvious about it. Making a chair out of steel tubes would have seemed roughly as promising as making one out of a pile of rocks. Breuer's cantilevered design accomplished the amazing feat of making steel graceful, elegant, and comfortable. He designed it as a young master at the Bauhaus—the extraordinary German art and design school that flourished under Henry van de Velde, Walter Gropius, Hannes Meyer, and Ludwig

Mies van der Rohe from 1902 until Mies shut it down under Nazi pressure in 1933. The Bauhaus made aesthetic discoveries that, like Breuer's chair, continue to shape everyday life.

A counterexample: machine beauty requires good functioning, and Bauhaus aesthetics dictate that houses have flat roofs. Flat roofs are much harder to weatherproof than pitched ones. So the typical Bauhaus residence was austerely elegant on the outside and the roof leaked, and the only possible verdict was "not beautiful."

The Hispano-Suiza cars of the 1920s and '30s were automotive deep beauty masterpieces. The coach-built bodies were lovely, the insides elegant and clever. "The engine was a showpiece in glossy black and aluminum," writes the car expert Ralph Stein; a seven-bearing crankshaft was "its loveliest jewel." Dynamic machine beauty and static shape-and-line loveliness reinforced each other. Picasso motored around the Riviera in a Hispano. "Passing his palm fondly along the hood," James Lord reports, the artist "said something proud about this vehicle, a recent acquisition, which he wanted us to admire."

The French Hispano was hand-built and fantastically expensive, but its beauty leaped to Detroit like a high-voltage spark. Alfred Sloan's first task as president of General Motors was to overtake Ford, and he hit on styling as an important weapon. In 1927 he hired Harley Earl to design a new GM car, a smaller, cheaper Cadillac called the La Salle. Earl simply transferred the Hispano's classy lines to the mass-market GM car.

The La Salle was a hit, and widely imitated throughout the American car industry. Earl was put in charge of GM's whole styling operation, and wielded huge influence over the whole U.S. car scene. Styling wasn't only a matter of looks. Good legroom, one-piece windshields, windshield wipers, and dome lights were all style issues in the early days. As automobiles matured, their shapes had to change for safety as much as aesthetic reasons: "as cars were driven more rapidly

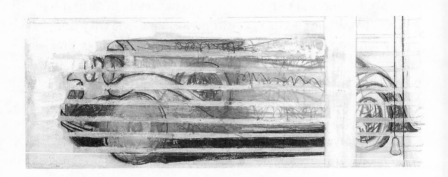

by more efficient motors," Sloan said, "it became dangerous to have vehicles with their center of gravity so far above the ground." Stylists were put in charge of making cars safer by making them lower. "An automobile stylist is an advocate of change," Sloan said on another occasion, "to a degree that was at first somewhat startling to production and engineering executives."

In artistic terms, the sort of industrial-design beauty we are discussing may sound shallow. Sometimes it is but sometimes not. One of the finest artworks of the century is the 1938 *J3* steam locomotive by Henry Dreyfuss for the New York Central's *20th Century Limited*. It has a great smooth hemispherical nose divided vertically by a fin down the middle, an elegant smooth cowl shielding the cow-catcher and pilot, solid driving wheels with punched-out holes for counterbalancing; every line serves a purpose, every detail is an indispensable part of the balanced whole, and the finished product has the loveliness of overwhelming power understated. The *J3* was sophisticated technology and it was beautiful. It remains beautiful. It is impossible to look at it without emotion. The precisionist artist Charles Sheeler showed its drivers, siderods, and piston assembly in his 1939 painting *Rolling Power*; merely transcribe the *J3*'s lines and you produced memorable art.

In science, beauty's role is less visible but at least as important as it is in technology. Physics amounts, fundamentally, to the act of examining two different-seeming phenomena and finding one underlying explanation. The search for beauty is intrinsic to physics: replace many small explanations with one big one and you achieve the simplicity of one account instead of many, the power of a far-reaching explanation instead of a bunch of narrow ones.

For example: throwing a ball and heating it in the oven are two very different events, and you can understand both in terms of the physical laws of moving objects. (In glancing at topics like this, I have no intention of passing myself off as a physicist—but the beauty of science, like the beauty of anything else, belongs to anyone who will sit still long enough to notice it.) When you heat an object, you make its constituent particles bounce around faster. When you notice its temperature rise, you are noticing the increased average bouncing-around speed of its particles. To study how balls behave when they move, bounce, and collide is to study, also, how objects behave when they are heated up—just direct your attention to very large numbers of very small balls and the physics of heated objects pops out like toast.

Physicists were bothered by the complexity of the physical laws governing subatomic forces and particles, the so-called standard model of the universe; it didn't set their tuning forks humming. (Beauty does cause an actual, physiological response—a response that psychologists and physiologists ought to study carefully. But, like almost everyone else, they shy away from aesthetic topics.) The unsatisfied physicists were driven to come up with a simpler, more beautiful explanation—and did, in the form of supersymmetry.

In the standard theory, "fermion"-type particles exert forces on each other that are mediated by "boson" types. Quarks, for example, are fermions; protons and neutrons are built of quarks—and then, moving up the size ladder, atomic nuclei are built out of protons and neutrons, atoms incorporate nuclei, molecules are made of atoms, sneakers of molecules, conceptual art sometimes includes sneakers, landfills incorporate conceptual art, and so on. Photons are a type of boson—photons being the carrier agents of electromagnetic energy, in the form of, for example, visible light.

Fermions and bosons are the only two basic types, but they each come in many varieties. Bosons create four basic forces, but the forces obey complex and arbitrary-seeming rules. Two are effective over long distances (electromagnetism and gravity), two over short distances (the strong and weak nuclear forces). Two are connected (electromagnetism and the weak nuclear force), but in the standard model the others don't seem to be—although they must be, ultimately. Two are registered Democrats but always vote Republican, two are Republicans who claim to hate cornflakes but are regularly seen leaving Stop & Shop with king-sized boxes of them. What are they *doing* with all these cornflakes? physicists wanted to know; it was all just too complicated. There had to be a simpler way.

Supersymmetry proposes one. It holds that each kind of boson must have a partner fermion and vice versa; granted that assumption, supersymmetry can describe the connections among all four basic forces and can describe, also, a primal Age of Symmetry when the universe was new and the four forces were symmetrical and there were no singing commercials even on MTV. That original, perfect symmetry required enormously high energies to maintain; the newborn universe was hot and full of beans and up to the task, but as it cooled, its energy level declined and full-blown symmetry disappeared—like a lasso collapsing from a perfect circle into a floppy swinging loop as a twirler's energy input declines.

No one had ever seen a "super-partner particle," as the partners dictated by supersymmetry are called, when the theory was dreamed up. Physicists invented them in the course of searching for a new, simple, beautiful theory of the universe. Having come up with the theory, they naturally set out to locate the objects whose existence the beauty of the universe demanded. Remarkably enough, they may indeed have spotted one, at Fermilab in Illinois. The data are new and in some ways evidently still unclear, but physicists are excited. Physicist to Partner Particle: "Beauty *required* that you exist!" Partner Particle: "Well, sir, here I am."

The beauty urge has always been a driving force in science and mathematics. Roger Penrose, the distinguished mathematical physicist, writes of the key idea in Kurt Goedel's famous theorem that it is "simple, beautiful, and profound." "To anyone who is motivated by anything beyond the most narrowly practical," writes the physicist J. R. Pierce, "it is worth while to understand Maxwell's equations simply for the good of his soul." Richard Feynman introduces a mathematical excursus in his physics text: "We could bring forth this formula in two minutes or so. . . . But science is as much for intellectual enjoyment as for practical utility, so instead of just spending a few minutes on this amazing jewel, we shall surround the jewel by its proper setting." "The most precise and beautiful definition of force imaginable might simply be . . . "

That art has entranced so many leading scientists is no accident—Einstein playing Bach on his violin, Jonas Salk and the architectural passion that led to Louis Kahn's Salk Institute. Insisting on the scientist-type versus artist-type distinction reflects the sort of dense bureaucratic worldview in which happiness hinges on everyone's keeping his three-ring binder neat. Frank Lloyd Wright was the greatest architect of the century, but his instinct for engineering was legendary. (Admittedly he perpetrated a few leaky roofs himself.) The analytic philosopher Ludwig Wittgenstein was an architect, too. The novelist Vladimir Nabokov was a lepidopterist on the side. It is the pride of creating beauty and the joy of feeling it that keeps the best scientists and technologists in business.

They make no secret of beauty's central role in their work, yet we act as if we don't believe them. They talk about beauty and we act as if they are kidding or humoring us. We are rarely willing to see machine beauty, no longer put machines (unless ironically) in the art we make, refuse to acknowledge (although it is right in front of our noses) the intellectual and spiritual closeness of art and science. Society's reaction to machine beauty brings Freudian resistance to mind. Metaphorically, I mean, but the metaphor is too apt to pass over. Some ideas we are happy to consider; others we push away as if instinctively. The art historian William Rubin speaks for many of us when he writes about the "almost unbridgeable gap between art and science in the modern world."

By insisting on the importance of aesthetics, do we ruin science by replacing its strong, hard foundations with soft, squishy ones? No. We say that beauty is subjective, and that's true up to a point but false beyond, and most of the action takes place beyond.

Science, first of all, is indeed a strong, hard, objective business, and in some ways fundamentally different from art. It has become fashionable in certain academic circles to hold that the truths of science are "socially constructed"—not absolutely true, only held to be true by the local authorities, dollars backed by official proclamation and not gold. The journal *Social Text*, for example, which is published by Duke University Press, devoted a recent issue to what it hopefully referred to as the Science Wars; the Press's executive director is the celebrated Duke English professor Stanley Fish. This particular issue is now famous on account of having accidentally included a parody article submitted by the physicist Alan Sokal. Sokal's intention was to lampoon the antiscience movement, but his piece turned out to be indistinguishable from "serious" scholarship—so far as the *Social Text* editors could tell, anyway. "Physical 'reality,' no less than social 'reality,' is at bottom a social and linguistic construct," Sokal wrote. And: "scientific 'knowledge,' so far from being objective, reflects and encodes the dominant ideologies and power relations of the culture that produced it." Sokal's parody was in keeping with Andrew Ross's introduction, evidently a nonparody. "The unjustified conferral of expertise on the scientist's knowledge of, say, chemical materials," Ross writes, "and not on the worker's or the farmer's experience with such materials, is an abuse of power that will not be opposed or altered simply by demonstrating the socially constructed nature of the scientist's knowledge."

Despite the antiscience cult's small size—it is probably no stronger on U.S. campuses than witchcraft or astrology— every scientist (and scholar and artist and citizen) has a duty to repudiate it. That the truths of science are "socially constructed" is false. Any child can see it is false; can see that the wavelength of blue light is the same in New York and Nigeria, that the valence of the oxygen in your body is the same whether you are male or female, that sine waves were shaped like sine waves yesterday afternoon and ten centuries ago. Of course, you could argue that the whole idea of wavelength is a cultural creation and that some people—ninth-century Catalonian wheelwrights, deconstructionist celebrity English professors—prefer to understand blue light in a wavelength-independent way, or not at all. But if so, they will have a hard time making sense of why the sky is blue, what the red-shifted spectrum of distant stars means, or why it is reasonable, given that we can see red and blue light, that we can also see orange but not radar or microwaves. Or don't they want to understand any of *that*, either? "Scientific truths are socially constructed" means only, if it means anything, that some people have better theories than other people.

But what about beauty? Beauty *must* be socially constructed, right? If you think so, you are forced to play down beauty's importance to science, because science is a unified, coherent whole. It coheres over centuries and millennia. We have relativistic quantum mechanics but still teach Newtonian mechanics, too. We have modern algebra but still need the old-fashioned kind. Mathematicians and scientists pose questions that remain interesting and are finally answered centuries later. Modern science incorporates discoveries going back to ancient Greece. If I believe that the beauty sense is a mere social construction, tumbled like trash before the passing breeze of fashion, I am forced to deny that it could possibly have inspired any such stunningly consistent, coherent intellectual structure as science and mathematics.

Many academics do believe, nowadays, that the beauty sense is "socially constructed," and many nonacademics agree—but that claim is largely false also. Fashions change, obviously, and tastes differ. And, yes, the rich, powerful, and prominent swing a lot of weight in the fashion department—always have and always will. Nothing new there. Here is what *is* surprising: picture a smelly, bedraggled twelfth-century French mason and his staggeringly foreign world—dangerous, ignorant, and wretchedly poor, muddy and filthy and sick, where there is no such thing as physiology, polyphonic music, or freedom, and life is tough and short even for the biggest cheeses. And yet that twelfth-century French mason finds Chartres cathedral compellingly beautiful (let's say he designed some of it), and so do we. Could anything *be* more amazing? Social constructivists are quick to point out that he doesn't read the cathedral the way we do, he feels it differently—but don't seem to understand how those facts only make the cathedral's depth of beauty *more* remarkable.

You could make the same observation about the Books of Samuel or the *Iliad* or the Ryoan-ji garden in Kyoto or a crowd of other masterpieces—and you would be struck in each case, I think, not by how greatly but how little beauty depends on social context.

I want to be fair to the social constructivists; how do they defend their views? Here is Garry Wills writing in *The New Yorker* about changing tastes in Homer translation:

So it is not true that the greatest works of art are timeless in their appeal. Masterpieces go neglected for long periods— as Gothic architecture did in the eighteenth century. Even the finest minds are limited by their historical circumstances. Thomas Jefferson literally could not *see* a Gothic cathedral, much less take it seriously. That is the problem with the claims for an immutable canon equally teachable in all times.

In the eighteenth century, granted, no one liked Gothic art. On the other hand, the great cathedrals we admire were admired, also, in 1950 and 1900 and 1850. That's a pretty fair run, isn't it? A hundred fifty years on the best-seller list? *Was* Jefferson's beauty sense so different from ours? The masterpieces he conceived—The Declaration of Independence and Monticello, the Virginia Statute for Religious Freedom and the University of Virginia—move us still. Jefferson read Homer and so do we. And the idea that the "canon" of great masterpieces is "immutable" and "equally teachable in all times" is idiotic on the face of it, and for exactly this reason we defenders of the canon do not believe it. It is hard to accept that Garry Wills even thinks we do. How many universities can he name where defenders of the canon insist on teaching Browning or Tennyson, say, because Browning and Tennyson were part of the 1920 canon? I can't stand Blake, although nowadays he is part of nearly everybody's canon. So what? We don't hold a canonical masterwork's appeal to be total and limitless, merely to be very damned great.

Wills has chosen to argue not with his opponents but with a caricature—you might almost say a spiteful caricature. Yet he is a first-rate thinker, scholar, and writer. So first-rate, you read his comments and despair for any chance of serious conversation across the culture chasm that divides us nowadays.

*   *   *

Beauty is crucial to software also. Most computer technologists don't like to discuss it, but the importance of beauty is a consistent (if sometimes inconspicuous) thread in the software literature. A 1996 essay collection edited by Terry Winograd, for example, brought together a series of papers focused on the proposition that design (as in "industrial design") is important to software. In the influential 1990 essay collection *The Art of Human-Computer Interface Design*, software prophet Ted Nelson claimed that "the integration of software cannot be achieved by a committee. . . . It must be controlled by dictatorial artists." In our 1990 programming language textbook, Suresh Jagannathan and I addressed "the enormous significance of aesthetics in the design of languages, indeed of software in general," and "the intimate connection between good engineering and aesthetic insight." Reflecting in 1978 on the seminal programming language Algol 60 that he helped design, Alan Perlis wrote that "this language proved to be an object of stunning beauty . . . a rounded work of art."

Beauty is more important in computing than anywhere else in technology. And where computers are concerned, the beauty paradox is especially acute.

Beauty is important in engineering terms because software is so complicated. Complexity makes programs hard to build and potentially hard to use; beauty is the ultimate defense against complexity. Beauty is our most reliable guide, also, to achieving software's ultimate goal: to *break free of the computer*, to break free *conceptually*. Software is stuff unlike any other. Cyberspace is unlike any physical space. The gravity that holds the imagination back as we cope with these strange new items is the computer itself, the old-fashioned physical machine. Software's goal is to escape this gravity field, and every key step in software history has been a step away from the computer, toward *forgetting* about the machine and its physical structure and limitations—forgetting that it can hold only so many bytes, that its memory is made of fixed-size cells, that you refer to each cell by a numerical address. Software needn't accept those rules and limitations. But as we throw off the limits, what guides us? How do we know where to head? Beauty is the best guide we have.

What *is* software? A running program is a kind of machine—a strange kind that gets power and substance from another machine, namely, the computer itself. An executing program is a machine that has been "embodied" by a computer in roughly the sense that a hand puppet is embodied when you slip your hand in. A nonexecuting program is the limp puppet without a hand, an empty shell. Slip a computer inside and it becomes a working software machine: an electric-powered information-transforming machine—in the sense that a clothes washer is an electric-powered clothes-transforming machine.

(If a running program is an information processor, does that mean it is just like the brain? After all, the brain is an information processor, too, right? Wrong: the brain is no mere information processor, it is a *meaning creator*—and meaning creation is a trick no computer can accomplish. The brain is a lump of hardware artfully arranged so as to produce an I—to create the illusion that some entity inside you is observing the world that your senses conjure up. That rose over there merely triggered, when you saw it, a barrage of neuron firings in your brain. But you have the sensation that some entity—namely, *you*, not to put too fine a point on it—actually *saw* the rose. Computers, so far as we can tell, are capable of no such trick. You can build a sophisticated digital rose-recognition system, wave a rose in front of it, and thereby bring about lots of electrical activity; and perhaps after a while some words will appear on a screen—"rose recognition accomplished" or "damn, what a rose!"—but no one and nothing has had the sensation of having *seen* anything. And no computer scientist has any reason to believe that any computer ever *will* have such a sensation, or any other sensation. Granted there is no reason in principle why you couldn't build a machine that shares with the brain this remarkable capacity; but there is also no reason to suppose you could do it without reproducing the brain itself.)

A running program is often referred to as a *virtual machine*—a machine that doesn't exist as a matter of actual physical reality. The virtual machine idea is itself one of the most elegant in technology history, and is a crucial step in the evolution of ideas about software. To come up with it, scientists and technologists had to recognize that a computer running a program isn't merely a washer doing laundry. A washer is a washer whatever clothes you put inside, but when you put a new program in a computer, it becomes a new machine.

The virtual machine idea clarifies an important problem— what exactly do programmers do? What activity are they engaged in when they make a program? Are they technical writers? (Their job is to compose what might be mistaken for technical documents.) Are they mathematicians? (The "documents" they create tend to be full of mathematical notation and might be mistaken for equations or proofs.) Neither: they are machine designers. They need talent and training of the sort that makes for structural engineers, automobile designers, or (in a general way) architects—not for writers or mathematicians. A program is a blueprint for a virtual machine—a blueprint that gets converted into the thing itself (the executing program, the "embodied" virtual machine) automatically when you hand it to a computer.

Here is a first entry in my guide to the nonexistent Museum of Beautiful Computing:

The virtual machine: *a way of understanding software that frees us to think of software design as machine design.*

Beauty is decisively important to computer technologists because, first, virtual machines are always in danger of drowning in complexity. Hardware machines are held in check by physical reality. Allow such a machine to get too complicated and no one will be able to afford it, or it will be so heavy it will stave in the floor, or use so much power it will burn up. But software builders don't need to assemble materials or worry about power supplies, heat dissipation, weight, drag, toxicity. So they go wild; a single programmer alone at his keyboard can improvise software machines of fantastic or even incomprehensible complexity. Imagine what kind of palaces people would live in if all you needed to do were to draw a blueprint, hand it to a machine, and see the structure realized automatically at the cost of a few drips of electricity. The most complex machines in the world today are made of software, and the "average" software machine—the typical word processor or spaceship game or operating system—is enormously complicated, too. A modern TV may contain half a million bytes of software (a byte is the size of a single alphabetical character inside the computer); a typical modern car has a 30,000-line program inside.

This huge complexity is responsible for software's permanent crisis: if you build a big enough program, it is almost impossible to make it come out right. Studies show that the average commercial software project takes 50 percent longer than it was supposed to, and one project in four is abandoned. Your only hope is to keep the number of serious bugs low enough so that your program is more or less okay most of the time. The "beta test" is the industry's admission of failure—the procedure whereby a product that is known to be flawed, but is nonetheless as good as the manufacturer can make it, is handed to expert users in hopes they will find some of the remaining bugs. (Beta testing was developed originally by kings, emperors, and potentates of the ancient world, whose field engineers would taste each dish on the menu before the big man tried it himself. If the taster keeled over, the beta test concept had proved itself yet again and a new tester was hired on the spot.)

A new airport is scheduled to open in Denver in the fall of 1993; fall '93 comes and goes, months pass, and it is still closed—because the software that is supposed to control the baggage-delivery system doesn't work. A Defense Department satellite tumbles into oblivion because of buggy software. In 1987 an announcement is made in California that two existing, correctly working programs will be merged— the driver registration and car registration systems—and some components added to allow people to use the finished product directly from kiosks. The new system is supposed to be finished by 1993. Then it is supposed to be finished by 1998. Then it is canceled, six years and forty some-odd million tax dollars after work began, because the task turns out to be in effect impossible. There are many similar stories.

To get out of the crisis, two steps are necessary: programmers need to be better trained, and software builders need to concentrate on making reusable blueprints and frameworks instead of reusable little pieces.

The first issue comes down in significant part to aesthetics. A good programmer can be a hundred times more productive than an average one, easily. The gap has little to do with technical or mathematical or engineering training, much to do with taste, good judgment, aesthetic gifts—and also, to be fair, a quality that has nothing to do with aesthetics: sheer intellectual aggressiveness. And brains don't hurt. But the fact that software's biggest hits are exactly the systems that are repeatedly praised for *elegance*—the Algol 60 language, from which so much modern practice derives; the "object-oriented" programming technique that emerged from Algol in 1967; the Apple desktop, on which the vast majority of computer users rely, in one form or other, today— ought to be a clue to the flummoxed industry that elegance has something to do with good software, that there is a connection somewhere between aesthetics and success.

But the beauty paradox is such that the industry *and* computer science researchers would far rather pursue mathematical solutions, so-called formal methods, than teach programmers about beauty. Mathematics is serious, aesthetics not; hence the field has been banging its head against the wall since the mid-1970s in an effort to put programming on a mathematical basis, and made such astonishingly little progress you'd imagine it would have drawn certain conclusions. But when mathematical methods fail, the invariable response is, "Bring on more mathematical methods!" A little progress has been made here and there, and mathematics is fine in its place. But it *cannot* be the whole story or even the main one, or we would not be stuck where we are, in a permanent mudbank spinning our wheels. "The hell with mathematics; let's teach our programmers about beauty" is what we ought to hear. Instead we are solemnly informed (in a representative *Scientific American* piece) that "intuition is slowly yielding to analysis as programmers begin using quantitative measurements. . . . The mathematical foundations of programming are solidifying."

"Anyone who wants to analyze the properties of matter in a real problem," Feynman writes,

> might want to start by writing down the fundamental equations and then try to solve them mathematically. [Who needs mere intuition when you can have *analysis*?] Although there are people who try to use such an approach, these people are the failures in this field [on second thought . . .]; the real successes come to those who start from a *physical* point of view, people who have a rough idea where they are going and then begin by making the right kind of approximations.

Perhaps there is something to be said for intuition after all. "The German emphasis on calculations," David Billington warns apropos of bridge building, "was a double-edged sword; it forced designers to think rationally but it also drew them away from forms for which they had no calculations, and thus narrowed the range of structural possibilities."

Not only is your typical software machine hugely complicated on the inside; it offers enormous power and a wide range of functions as well. A taste for beauty is the technologist's most important ally, also, in his struggle to produce software that people are capable of using effectively.

Beauty determines which virtual machines triumph and which are rejected, left to rust like old cars in weedy meadows. Ugly virtual machines waste the underlying computer's power and, vastly more important, the user's time, but a beautiful program hovers nearby like an attentive, unobtrusive British butler. A beautiful program's way of doing things is so close to your own that creative symbiosis develops, a thought-amplifying feedback loop. You have an idea and the machine accommodates it immediately—no backtalk, no bargaining. The machine's transparency and willingness might even nudge your thinking a step forward.

The software's role is humble and basically passive, but it can amplify your thought—an important accomplishment. One of the field's foremost visionaries, the inventor in the late 1960s of the mouse and the computer window, ran a laboratory with the strange title Augmentation Research Center. According to Douglas Engelbart, computers are tools for "augmenting human intellect."

They can play that role, however, only to the extent they are beautiful. No creative symbiosis is possible with an ugly virtual machine—with a complex or weak program that forces you to bend to its worldview instead of accommodating yours.

In the computer world, beauty is the most important thing there is, and the paradox is this: beauty inspires the best technologists and confuses or outright repels everyone else—at least to begin with.

Ordinary technologists don't understand it, and often behave as if they hate it. They don't, actually; it's just that fancy features and complex, sophisticated functions inspire them—and, as for beauty, they can't see it at all. Because they are unaware of it, they will knock it over and destroy it without batting an eyelash, utterly oblivious.

The public's relationship to beautiful software is more complicated. "Almost no one seems to be able to recognize *good* design," writes Nelson—"except users, and that only sometimes." Not sometimes, *always*—but only in the long term. Consumers invariably go for beauty in the end; right up to that point, many seem to detest it. Why? It is a hard question and no one knows for certain. I will discuss it in these pages. This much is clear: (1) most computer technologists are oblivious to beauty; (2) the best are obsessed with it; (3) the public has a love-hate relationship with beauty in computing; and (4) beauty is the most important quality that exists in the computer world, when all is said and done.

To see this paradox in action, consider the strange story of Apple computers.

≡TWO

The Paradox of Beauty

Early in 1996 the Apple computer company ran into deep trouble. It managed to lose seven hundred million dollars in a single quarter, which is more than most businesses *earn* their whole lives. The company's very survival was in danger, and economists, businessmen, and technology pundits were at a loss. Apple computers, after all, were famous for elegance; the Macintosh was the computer with the "extremely elegant operating system," one computer magazine explained in 1984, the year of the Mac's birth. Elegance made these computers easy to set up, use, maintain, and generally get along with. Because Apple had done its job so well, the Macintosh (furthermore) attracted good software the way Marilyn Monroe attracted qualified suitors.

"The really fine software has always been on the Mac," the CEO of a software-engineering firm pointed out in 1996, "because the Mac developer community understands ergonomic design and ease-of-use." But Apple's beautiful computers were losing to Microsoft-equipped machines—and

Microsoft, it was generally agreed, couldn't care less about beauty. Microsoft cares about beauty (dazed pundits could be overheard muttering to each other, wherever dazed pundits congregate) the way clams care about pantyhose. Why was beauty losing? What did its defeat mean?

Apple computers were beautiful in the classic technology sense, simple and powerful. They were attractive in an important area: the machine's "operating system" or (to put it another way) "interface" or "dashboard" was elegant. "Apple's Macintosh offers a superior user interface that attracts passersby," one computer magazine wrote in 1984 with only the barest hint of condescension. No matter what applications you run, a computer undertakes to accomplish certain basic tasks: keep your files and documents in order, run the applications you tell it to, move information into and out of the machine. Those basic functions are the operating system's responsibility. Because the operating system is the boss program, it is also the program you deal with whenever you are trying to get something done. So the operating system decides the computer's look and feel. Imagine your computer as a ratty armchair; the operating system is the slipcover. It defines the human-computer meeting point or *interface*, where rubber meets road, where chair meets derrière.

Apple's "desktop"-style operating system is one of the key inventions of computing history. In the desktop approach, the computer screen is a stylized representation of a paper-covered desk: many documents can be visible simultaneously, each in a separate "window." To manipulate documents you move them in a fairly simple, natural way around the computer screen. You tell the computer what to do by selecting the right entry in a "menu" of choices.

When the Macintosh appeared, its main competitor was Microsoft's DOS system, which was more complicated and less powerful than the Mac. In DOS, you communicated with the machine by typing sometimes arcane instructions one line at a time, and the computer screen was a stylized representation of nothing. "Many users have problems re-membering the syntax of even the common DOS 'house-keeping' commands," a computer magazine noted in 1989; "it only gets worse for those more useful but esoteric com-mands."

The desktop idea allowed you to do things yourself instead of telling the computer how to do them, and helped you maintain a sense of context and the big picture. If you wanted to select an electronic document to work on or print or throw out, you pointed to the document on-screen the way you would reach out and grab it in the physical world; in DOS you had to type instructions to the computer telling *it* which document to select. The main intellectual challenge of life in general is remembering context, keeping the big pic-ture in mind; the Apple desktop allowed you to keep a bunch of documents or tasks in view simultaneously, where DOS directed your attention to one only.

How do we know, however, that the desktop's good points constitute beauty and not just good, solid, rational design? If the Apple desktop is beautiful, how about the average mi-crowave oven, automatic transmission, TV set, beer can?

You know beauty when you feel it; there is no way to *demonstrate* its presence. What we *can* do, though, is point out some of the telltales of simplicity and power.

For example: although the key ideas of the Apple desktop are not at all obvious, people tend to grasp them immediately and learn readily how to use them. A computer screen is tiny compared to an actual desktop; the computer version can ac-commodate a decent amount of material because of the "icon" mechanism—a window can be collapsed into a small symbol; the symbol can be reinflated again, back to full size. There is no analogy to that sort of crumpling-uncrumpling operation in the physical world, yet people tend to grasp quickly what an icon is and how it works.

Icons are used for other purposes also—for example, to bring the file-cabinet, trash-can, and plug-in peripherals onto the computer desktop. Again, people tend to grasp readily (except in a few unfortunate cases, having to do, for example, with some weird inconsistencies surrounding the trash-can symbol) what these are for. It's the same story with other key aspects of the design—pull-down menus, say; they are new and powerful inventions with no physical analogs, but people tend to grasp them quickly.

The parts are blended, furthermore, into an aesthetically pleasing whole: Apple's desktop has a disciplined visual richness that is characteristic of fine design. The eye wants variety, not sameness, but it also wants a clean underlying beat so that it can sense the big picture and not be overwhelmed by complexity. This is the design principle I called *espalier* in an earlier book. Ludwig ("less is more") Mies van der Rohe wanted visual richness in his famous Barcelona pavilion—so he built walls of onyx and green Tinian marble, and reflecting pools lined with black glass, but he boxed the rich veining of the stone and the water's complex chop into rigid rectangles and thereby subordinated them to the building's overall rhythm. The result was clean, clear elegance, sharp as lemon juice. You experience the color of the stained glass at Chartres with such overwhelming vividness in part because it is disciplined, like a dancer moving to the beat, by the regular shapes and spacing of the window surrounds.

Espalier is the central design principle of serious music: the complexity of a tonic theme and dominant countertheme, for example, struggling hand to hand inside the neatly laid-out flowerbeds of sonata form. A crazy profusion of skyscrapers boxed into a rigid street grid makes Manhattan one of the most visually exciting (and tensest) spots on earth. Apple's desktop is an artistic success for the same underlying reasons. The icons and windows are all different, but they obey the same underlying rules and are neatly laid out on the screen. The same fonts and drawing styles and mouse choreographies apply in each case.

(A person might complain, legitimately, that invoking

Chartres to praise Apple is like cheering up your depressed poodle by presenting him with a gold Rolex, when you know perfectly well that a can of Alpo would have done the trick. But the point is not to equate these two achievements, rather to point out that when a computer display is beautiful, it owes its beauty to the same deep principles that hold at Chartres.)

It has many flaws and is a long way from *great* art, but Apple's desktop is modestly beautiful beyond question. (I will describe some of the flaws later.) Discussing the thing in aesthetic terms is no mere academic conceit, either. It is beautiful because the technologists who built it aimed to make it beautiful, and thought of themselves as artists. They signed the mold for the computer's plastic housing; their signatures appeared inside every one of the original upright Macs. When Steve Jobs, who led the design team, wanted to inspire his people to finish up expeditiously, he told them "real artists ship" (or in other words: don't dawdle, get the product out the door).

The Apple desktop: simple and powerful insofar as it lets you pick your way through the unfamiliar terrain of the world inside the computer by following your real-world, physical-document instincts.

But if the Macintosh was beautiful and beauty mattered, what was happening? What had gone wrong? Why had the battle between Apple and Microsoft turned into a rout? Enter the beauty paradox.

Some people explained Apple's desperate condition in terms of path dependence, an economic theory that emerged in the 1980s; good products are defeated by bad ones, path dependence explains, on account of bad luck. (This may possibly not strike you as the deepest theory you've ever heard, but at least it's pithy. Perhaps the economists who invented it might one day give birth to another theory explaining that, fundamentally, the reason poverty exists is that some people don't have enough money. This may explain why they call economics the dim science, or the grim science, or the glum science, or whatever they call it.) (And what do they call computer science? Don't ask.) "The best don't always win," one economics writer explains; "economists are discovering the disorder that lurks in the shadows of their simple, elegant models of capitalist progress."

Bad products are successful, the theory goes on to explain, because they are at the right place at the right time. Some observers have gone so far as to claim that, contrary to what everyone had believed, Apple's problems prove that beauty *doesn't* matter after all. "Computer boxes are—computer boxes," a technology writer pointed out tautologically in *The New Republic*. Hence whether the systems they run are beautiful or ugly doesn't matter. The article took Apple to task for making a big deal about "elegance," a word it placed in dunce-cap quotation marks so that everyone could see how useless it was. If "elegance" were important, ugly Microsoft wouldn't be defeating elegant Apple.

These explanations were wrong. We didn't need "path dependence" to explain why bad ideas sometimes win, or *The New Republic* to alert us to the unimportance of beauty—for a reason that was obvious to many a clever halibut: Microsoft was beating Apple with Apple's own ideas. By 1996 Microsoft had long since become a fervent Apple convert. In 1990 it had scored a huge success with a product called Windows 3.0; the point of that product was precisely to make IBM-style computers with clunky, old-fashioned DOS operating systems behave like svelte Apple Macintoshes. *Consumer Reports* laid it on the line: Windows 3.0 is a "Macintosh-style system designed to run on a DOS-based computer." "Microsoft," the *New York Times* reported, is "the company whose software gives computers the same functions that the Apple Macintoshes do and that has proven adept at imitating each Apple innovation and then capturing most of the market." When Windows 3.0 swept the world, so did Apple's concept of beautiful software. That didn't do Apple stockholders any good, but the Macintosh designers were entitled to feel vindicated.

Pushing beauty instead of old-fashioned DOS ugliness, Microsoft emerged as the uncontested leader of the desktop computing world. In part that was because, pre–Windows 3.0, Microsoft had been the leader in operating systems but not in applications—other companies made the leading DOS spreadsheets, word processors, databases. Windows forced everyone to go back and start over, and Microsoft itself emerged (surprise!) as the leading Windows application supplier.

But that victory couldn't have happened if Windows 3.0 itself hadn't been such a massive boffo hit. Three years after its release, Microsoft had sold twenty-five million copies. It was only during the fourth year of Macintosh production, in 1987, that Apple assembled its *one* millionth Mac. Windows 3.0 was such a success that by 1993, sales of Windows software exceeded sales of Apple and DOS software put together. Choosing between Apple and DOS forced a user to consider many factors. But once you had chosen DOS you faced, come 1990, a new and simpler choice; to stay in the DOS world or switch to Windows. That decision hinged on aesthetics alone. You didn't *need* to switch; Microsoft continued to support DOS and bring out new releases, and there were plenty of DOS applications for sale, and DOS "shells" that smoothed out some of the rough spots without going to a Mac-style interface.

Beauty wins in the end. Still, there is a hard problem here. Why did Microsoft win with Apple's beautiful idea? Why didn't *Apple* win with it?

Microsoft got a boost out of Windows 3.0 that turned the whole industry upside down—but Microsoft had been enormously successful before Windows, too. By late 1986 the Mac and the Microsoft-equipped IBM PC had both had a chance to make their pitches, and "I.B.M. computers," the *New York Times* wrote, "dominate corporate desktops." The fingers-crossed headline of a 1988 Apple advertisement summed things up: "MIS manager buys Macintosh, keeps job." In the corporate world especially, the world of Management Information Services, Macintosh sales never even came close to Microsoft's. How could ugly DOS have done so well against the beautiful Mac? It is a hard question precisely because we know that the public is *not* indifferent to beauty— Windows 3.0 appeared and Microsoft pulled away from the pack. ("Users of DOS PCs rejoice!" a computer magazine gushed when 3.0 appeared; "rarely does an operating-system upgrade render existing hardware so much more useful.") But how come Microsoft and not Apple was ahead *beforehand*?

In part because Windows brought the price of elegance down. DOS computers were cheaper than Macintoshes because DOS had been designed originally for the IBM PC, and IBM had allowed "clone" companies to copy the PC and sell their own versions. Coke and Super-Cheep Cola don't taste the same but the clones and the IBM PC did, and the clone companies tended to sell their machines for less than IBM charged. Competition forced IBM to keep its prices down, too; Apple, on the other hand, kept Macintosh prices high.

Some people who wanted Apple-style elegance couldn't afford it until Microsoft made it available on the cheap. The great thing about Microsoft Windows was that it had "most of the Macintosh's advantages"—*Consumer Reports* again— "for less money."

Yet this explanation is not wholly satisfying. In the Microsoft world, the rush to Windows and away from DOS was overwhelming; but in the pre-Windows world, Macs hadn't cost *that* much more than DOS machines. (The usual price difference was well under 50 percent.) Given Windows's proven drawing power, why shouldn't the Mac's version of that same idea have attracted larger crowds? The question becomes more perplexing when you consider that, however appealing Windows seemed, the Mac ought to have seemed *more* appealing. Windows 3.0 was Mac-like and a huge step beyond DOS, but most experts agreed that it fell short of the real thing. "The Macintosh operating system," according to a *New York Times* technology columnist in 1991, "is better than the Microsoft Corporation's Windows 3.0." That categorical judgment is typical.

More perplexing still: studies published during the pre-Windows era suggested that, although a Mac cost more than a DOS machine, it was cheaper in the long run because it was so much easier to use and maintain. A Mac-style graphical interface "generates a greater return on information technology investment than a traditional [DOS-style] interface," one independent study concluded; this particular study was publicized by *Microsoft* after Windows 3.0 appeared. According to studies like this, people who bypassed the Mac for DOS were actually *paying extra for ugliness*.

How did ugliness manage to dominate the game for so long?

For many reasons, having to do with prices and advertising, IBM and the clones, marketing and personalities. We can account for most of what happened on those terms—but not quite all. Stack up all the obvious explanations, climb aboard, stand on tiptoe, and you still can't *quite* reach the cookie jar. When you consider the machine's intuitive appeal ("a lot of people bought the Mac," a software executive said in 1986, "because it was so amazing") *plus* the cost-benefit studies that came down in the Mac's favor ... okay, Microsoft won—but in a rout? And so a person is forced to wonder: Is it possible that, right up to the moment people fell in love courtesy of Microsoft with Apple-style beauty, they were repelled by it?

Yes, it is possible. Have a look at the Macintosh journalism of the 1980s. A certain word leaps out repeatedly.

"When many potential buyers look at the Mac, they will first be struck by its . . . cuteness" (1984). "In the beginning, there was that cute Mac with the smiling face" (1988). "When the cute little Macintosh first knocked on the door more than three years ago . . . " (1988). "Too bad there's nothing like 1–2–3 on that little thing . . . it's so cute!" (1987). "That's not because Mac's cute, although it is . . . " (1984). "I have never liked mice, except for Mickey. OK, so they are sort of small and cute . . . " (1984). "Most DOS shells are character-oriented. They don't use those cute little icons . . . " (1988). "Who wants cute?" (an industry trade newspaper headline, 1984). Add it all up and here is what you get: compared to the Macintosh, writes unusually frank and brave technology columnist John Dvorak in 1984, a DOS-equipped IBM PC is "a man's computer designed by *men* for men."

You got it: beautiful technology is *unmanly*. Anyway, lots of people think so. How to say it if you're less brave than Dvorak? Easy. Pat it on the head and call it cute. But Henry Ford never beat around the bush. Mr. Ford "had no use for beauty on a machine, and questioned the masculinity of those who insisted on putting it there." Apple actually *encouraged* the pat-me-on-the-head approach, a deep and devastating mistake.

Technology—of course!—is a man's world, and beauty messes it up totally. Henry Ford is absolutely clear on this point: *elegance is sissy.* Men who want to seem manly, women who want to seem competent—elegance gives everyone the creeps.

To pay money for elegant technology is to seem unserious, self-indulgent, and arguably incompetent. "Because the Macintosh was so easy to use, people concluded it wasn't powerful," Apple executive Guy Kawasaki complained in 1988. "The users of those business Macs," a computer magazine wrote in 1987, "certain they'd seen a better idea at work, had gone out on a limb to buy them, and often had taken a lot of hard-edged joshing." "Of course there are many technically sophisticated people who are not going to be bothered by the cuteness of the Macintosh," according to a trade newspaper in 1984—and, of course, many others *were* going to be bothered.

Dvorak's column was an unusual exercise in straightforwardness. Cards like these are rarely laid on the table. But you catch a glimpse in automobile history of popular attitudes toward elegant, user-friendly technology. Hindsight gives us a clearer view of the period—which was also, as it happens, more honest than ours. Even the finagling blather of its advertisements was more on the level.

Thus the electric starter motor was marketed, when it appeared in 1912, as "the ladies' aid." Ladies did tend to have trouble crank-starting an engine. Many gentlemen did too, and hand-cranking was an unmitigated nuisance for everybody. But the starter got filed under female technology from the beginning and, although the classification might have been nonsense, at least people were honest about what it *was*.

Could there be a connection between the marketing of starter motors eighty-odd years ago and Apple computers today? I can't prove it (it's not a provable-type proposition), but it is impossible not to wonder. Closed cars were marketed as a boon to women; "heaters, air conditioning, and automatic transmissions," writes historian James Flink, "were innovated with the ladies in mind." I mentioned Harley Earl and his General Motors Styling Section; the "beauty parlor" is what other ranking GM executives called Earl's operation. His stylists were the "pretty-picture boys."

Microsoft's introducing Windows, my guess is, registered with the public in the manner of John Wayne endorsing handbags for gentlemen, and carrying one himself. Microsoft got famous selling serious, ugly software, outfitting the "man's computer designed by *men* for men." The company was equipped in Nixon-to-China fashion to make elegance legitimate in a way Apple never was.

My Webster's *Second International* holds that "bold," "daring," and "undaunted" are synonyms for "manly," and so of course the story is ironic, because (strictly on empirical grounds) the popular belief at its base is wrong. I have never known a bold, daring, undaunted programmer to prefer the PC to the Macintosh. I don't claim that there *are* no such programmers, only that I have never met or heard about any. The champion programmers I know all favor either Unix or the Mac. Curiously (just as an aside), many of the century's most original aesthetic leaders, from Pablo Picasso and Frank Lloyd Wright through Harley Earl himself, were macho almost to the point of self-parody. The machoest operators often seem to care most about beautiful technology. The beauty of classic race cars largely reflects race drivers' love of beautiful cars. Ralph Nader isn't greatly moved by beauty in automobiles, so far as one can tell; David E. Davis is.

Masculine versus feminine can't account for the whole beauty paradox. But it offers a seductive explanation for one piece of it.

Of course, when you are dealing with aesthetics you are dealing, ultimately, with taste and sensibility and education and genes and whimsy; whatever the consensus, some people simply won't understand. When you tell them, "Look, it's beautiful!" they will answer "Why?" (And you will tell them, "Oh, never mind, the hell with it. Great weather today!") In the piece I mentioned earlier, *The New Republic* congratulates Apple's new CEO, Gil Amelio, because he "does not appear to have the same sentimental attachments to the purism of Apple's past" as his predecessors. He suffers from no silly infatuation with (heads up, watch the quotes!) "elegance." Back in the real world, the release of beauty-for-the-masses in the unlikely form of Windows 3.0 created "a new world order with Microsoft at the helm," according to a 1991 headline in *Marketing Computers*. "With Windows 3.0's success, Microsoft Corp. now dominates the PC software industry." And

Harley Earl's styling shop was crucial to General Motors's superseding Ford and dominating the U.S. car industry for half a century.

Except when it is bringing about new world orders, beautiful technology hardly matters at all.

⊟THREE

The Aesthetics of Computer Science

The technology community distrusts beauty and tries to ambush it wherever it appears. The most beautiful idea in the history of software was captured in the programming language called Algol 60. Technologists reacted to its elegance like sharks to blood in the water. Algol 60 kicked off a language-design frenzy that produced such grossly complex successor languages as PL/I and Algol 68. In the 1970s a few inspired computer scientists went back to their Shaker workshops and came up with updated but still elegant versions of Algol 60—a new generation of simple, powerful languages like Pascal and C. New feeding frenzies ensued, and Pascal and C begat a new crop of complex, ugly beasts; and the process continues.

Recently a language called Java, developed by JavaSoft and Sun Microsystems, has attracted enormous attention, owing partly to its being computer science's latest return to Walden Pond—its latest try at capturing today's important program-building mechanisms in a simple package. More important still are the simplicity and elegance of Java's basic premise: instead of writing programs for some particular computer, you write them using Java for a nonexistent computer (the Java Virtual Machine) that *every* computer can become if it aspires to be, simply by assuming the Java Virtual Machine's identity. The original computer thereby disappears, no longer matters. Instead of building a program for some particular computer, you build one using Java for any and all computers that are willing to disguise their identities inside the Java Virtual Machine. A beautiful idea, simple and powerful. But whatever Java's fate, one thing is certain: mediocre technologists will be driven—they can't help it—to take this elegant system and mess it up. New and more complicated turbo-Javas are guaranteed to appear.

Most technologists act as if they hate beauty. It is no secret what makes for good software; when a computer magazine praises some PC application for being "useful because of its elegant simplicity," it builds on an assumption that is nearly universal among software consumers, even if they don't apply it consistently. Make it elegant. Keep it simple. Yet, as software progresses from version to version, successive upgrades typically "convert simple programs into giant software monoliths," writes the astronomer, author, and computer expert Clifford Stoll. When a technologist dreams up a new "feature," some new function that might be carried out by an existing program, his inclination is to glue it right on. A roomful of software developers would remind you of the nursery-school scene where children are making collages out of all the glitter and sparkles and fancy buttons and gaily painted macaroni they can grab, and you can smell the Elmer's glue a mile off. The children will likely be happy and absorbed, and software developers tend to feel the same way under corresponding circumstances. Their gleeful faces are a sight to behold. You want to hug each and every one of them, and toss the finished product in the trash. Why do they do it? They know they shouldn't. Their bosses know they shouldn't. It's a paradox.

"'Featuritis,'" Ted Nelson writes, "is a principal and well-known disease of software. . . . The disease of featuritis is the unclarity and confusion that results from *having too many separate, unrelated things to know and understand* [his italics]. . . . Ultimately, the best software design assimilates all its functions to a few clear and simple principles." This matter of "a few clear and simple principles" is a crucial aesthetic goal. The successful pursuit of simplicity and power leads to integration, *unification*. The wonderful thing about Harley Earl's 1927 La Salle, Alfred Sloan explained, was that it had "the unified appearance we were looking for." One historian defines the goals of the streamlined style of the 1930s—one of the strongest, most original design movements in American history—as the "unification of formerly uncoordinated elements."

Stoll lists some fancy and, so far as he is concerned, useless features that arrived with a new version of Microsoft's "Word" program—for example, he can now include video clips and voice announcements in his documents, two things every author is dying to do. Clearly Microsoft's president, Bill Gates, has big plans in mind (but we knew that already). For if authors can add voice to their documents, it won't be long before every book will be capable of saying (in a mild, scholarly voice), "Turn the page, stupid!" when it senses readers nearing the bottom. It won't be long before corporate annual reports are configured so that, whenever three copies come into physical contact, they all break out into *Besame Mucho* together, so heartily that stockholders immediately forget any bad feelings about corporate earning. A more valuable new word-processor feature is inconceivable, except for a "translate designated text-block into Pig Latin" command, which I understand Microsoft is working on.

"Were these useless features simply add-on whistles," Stoll writes, "I'd shrug. But I've paid someone to develop and test this code, and it's wasting space on my disk drive, not to mention slowing down my computer. . . . I'm happy to sacrifice functionality for simplicity, reliability, and, especially, ease of learning." But the average technologist yearns to make things complicated, not simple. Elsewhere Stoll asks, still on the same topic, "Microsoft needs a thousand pages to describe a popular program, written for ordinary people? Am I expected to know all this just to write a letter to my friend Gloria?"

For the computing I do at my office, I am stuck with a large technology company's version of Unix and a window system called Open Windows. The Open Windows system comes with certain functions built in. Like many other systems, it can, for example, display a clock face in a window, and update it once a minute so the hands always show the right time—a neat and useful trick. But not long ago a new version of Open Windows arrived, and when I turned the computer back on I discovered that my clock face window now had the words "US/Eastern" blazoned across the bottom, with no way to get rid of them. Now here is an invaluable new feature: I must say to myself (I don't know) five or six times a day on average, "Where am I, anyway? San Francisco? Kuala Lumpur?" But thanks to this new feature, I can always look at my clock display and be reminded. And of course it happens regularly to all of us that we catch sight of a clock and wonder, "Sure, it's 9 A.M. someplace, but *where*?" In short, I have acquired ten useless new characters permanently stuck to my screen—desktop litter, the electronic equivalent of trash on the sidewalk. And some software designer somewhere, formerly the kind of sanctimonious twelve-year-old who *always* kept his three-ring binder neat, is grinning triumphantly.

When I am working on a laptop, the program that prints my draft copies doesn't put "1," "2," "3," on successive sheets; it has got to print "*page* 1," "*page* 2," "*page* 3," lest I mistake those mysterious page-top numbers for recommended lottery picks and lose a bundle. You wish software like this came with a rear end so you could kick it. Add *that* to your list of great features for the next release, software houses of the world!

The impulse to compromise technology by adding useless features is hardly restricted to software builders. Typical American slice of life: I am alone in the house with a new AT&T answering machine, which has recently been through the emotional turmoil of a power failure. Someone calls; I am busy and let the machine pick up; a message is dictated. Soon after, I learn the awful truth: after a power failure, the thing resets itself in beep mode. An unplayed message causes the machine to bleat like a wounded goat until the recording is played or you shoot out the bleeper with a pistol. My wife set the thing up originally, and I have no idea how it is done and don't care (she has far more patience for badly designed machines, and also for everything else, than I do); pushing every switch on the front panel yields no clue. AT&T's official corporate strategy at this point calls for me to drop everything, hunt down the owner's manual, and curl up for a good read—and when I finally trace down the "How to Turn Off Bleating" section, it probably just says, "Find a pistol and shoot out the bleeper." In any case, I have other things to do—and so, naturally, I turn the damned thing off, and days pass before we remember to turn it back on. AT&T's industrial-design skills seem to be about average; maybe better.

I recently bought a new Sony VCR. When you slip in a tape that can only be played, not recorded—a commercial video, for example—this obnoxious machine (and other brands are just as bad) starts playing it automatically—although you don't *ever* want the tape to start when you load it; you want it to start when you're seated and ready to watch. When you shut this VCR off, it smirkily retunes the cable box to the channel you were watching when you turned it on.

But when you shut off the VCR, your intention is to shut off the VCR, not switch channels. Minor annoyances, of course. But technology's single most important obligation is *to get out of the way.* The point of machinery is to make life easier; useless features and bad design make technology a self-important nuisance instead of a help.

The geniuses of the computer field, on the other hand, are the people with the keenest aesthetic senses, the ones who are capable of creating beauty. Beauty is decisive at every level: the most important interfaces, the most important programming languages (the tools a person uses to build interfaces), the winning algorithms (the computing methods that underlie every piece of software) are the beautiful ones.

Computer science is scientific insofar as it has a theoretical foundation that allows a person to make general statements and prove them. Theoretical computer science is founded on a mathematical invention that is the quintessence of simplicity and power, the Turing machine first described in a seminal paper by the English mathematician Alan Turing. Turing's work had many consequences, one of which was to set computer science on a beautiful foundation.

Turing wanted to prove statements about what can be computed in principle versus what can't ever be, no matter what. His central paper was published in 1936, before anything resembling a modern digital computer existed. (Turing himself helped develop the modern computer during the Second World War.) But you could investigate the theoretical capacities of a general-purpose computer even if you couldn't buy one, and Turing proceeded to do so. In order to carry out his investigations, he needed to say what a "computing machine" was. He described one of stunning simplicity. Eventually he and a group of other mathematicians came to believe an amazing thesis about his simple machine: that it was capable of computing anything that *could* be computed.

The simple machine worked like this: imagine a tape ruled

algorithm is something along these lines: grab the first word in the document; look it up in a dictionary; if you can't find it and can't figure out how it might have been formed from some other word you *can* find, then alert the user to a possible spelling error. Repeat for the next word, and continue until you reach the end.

Algorithms are the heart of software. Apple couldn't have built its desktop unless it had algorithms for drawing windows on the screen, turning windows into icons, responding to mouse clicks, and so on through a long list. In many cases, appropriate algorithms already existed, and it was merely a matter of capturing them in software. In some cases, algorithms had to be invented.

A good algorithm has to be powerful: has to function well, which usually means running fast and not requiring too much memory. The best algorithms are simple, too: a simple algorithm is easier to capture in software—easier to program correctly, to understand, analyze, and improve. In short, the best algorithms are the beautiful ones.

One of the most beautiful in computing, for example, was invented by the English scientist C. A. R. Hoare (who is today at Oxford) in 1962. It is called Quicksort, and it solves this problem: you are given an unsorted list; sort it. The list might consist of words to be alphabetized, numbers to be arranged from smallest to largest, or anything similar.

Suppose you are given a stack of index cards with a number written on each and asked to sort it. Here is one obvious algorithm, called "insertion sort": you look at the second card in the stack; if its number is smaller than the top card's, put it first. If it is larger, leave it. Then go to the third card and stick it on top or in the second position or leave it, depending on *its* number. Then go to the fourth card, and continue in this way until you reach the bottom.

Hoare's Quicksort works differently. Remove the top card. Say the number on that card is 117. Now go through the rest of the deck and, for each card you meet, stick it on top of 117 if its number is smaller than 117, beneath if its number is greater. Your deck is now sorted into three groups—cards that are less than 117, 117 itself, and cards that are greater than 117. Repeat this procedure on the top and bottom groups. The old top group is now split into three itself around some "pivot card," and likewise the old bottom group. Repeat the procedure again for each new group. Repeat it again for each of *those* new groups, and so on, until each group consists of one card; and you're done.

Here is what happened. You split the deck into a "small-numbers" and a "big-numbers" group; then you split the small-numbers group into small small numbers and big small numbers, and so on. You repeatedly swept through the deck, dropping each card into an ever-smaller top or bottom pile.

Now let's roughly compare the two algorithms. Let's say you are insertion-sorting and are finished except for the last card in the deck. How much work do you face in handling this last card? To find out where it goes, you need to examine the deck card by card starting at the top. In the worst case, the card that was at the bottom actually *belongs* on the bottom, but you don't know that until you have looked at every other card in the whole deck. If the deck is n cards big, you needed to examine essentially all n (actually only $n-1$, but call it n) before finding a home for the bottom card. If we call examining a card "one operation," placing that last card required n operations.

On average, you won't need to examine all n cards to insert that last one; you will need to examine only about half the cards, half n. To insert the second-to-last card, you would need to examine one card fewer, on average, and so on, as you go backward through the deck. But we say that insertion sort is an "n-squared" algorithm—it requires about n-squared operations, roughly speaking. The reasoning goes like this: "you needed around n operations to handle that last card, and there are n cards in the deck—let's say you need around n operations for each one of them; so you wind up with n times n operations in all, n operations for each of n cards, or n squared." Actually you examine only around *half n* for the last card, on average, but half n is close to n, as scientists count things (n to the fifth power is a long way from n, but half n is close). And to sort the *average* card in the deck, the one right in the middle, you probably needed to examine only around one-quarter n; but again, that's not far from n, roughly speaking.

So we have an n-squared algorithm. To sort a deck of a hundred cards, you need roughly ten thousand operations. To sort a deck of a million, you need roughly a trillion operations.

Quicksort is much faster on average. You remove the top card and split the deck into cards that are smaller and cards that are larger than this top one; if the top card was an "average" number, you will have split the deck into roughly equal pieces—about half the cards are smaller and half are larger than the average card. Then you repeat the splitting operation on each new group, and so on. Let's suppose you continue, by luck, to find average cards on top of each new group. How many times do you go through the deck splitting groups until you're finished? The first split yields two groups of around half n cards each; the next split yields four of around a quarter n each; the next yields eight of around an eighth n each; how many splits until you wind up with groups of *one* card each? The answer is log-to-the-base-2 of n: you get n when 2 is raised to this power. Suppose the deck is sixteen cards long: the first split yields two groups of 8, split 2 yields four groups of 4, split 3 yields 8 groups of 2, split 4 yields 16 groups of 1. We needed 4 splits; 2 to the 4th power is 16. Or, in the words of the immortal Gershwin song, "I got logarithm, I got music, I got my man, and I really enjoy doing trigonometry." You in the back, pay attention.

Now. We needed approximation to reach this number, but it gives us the right general idea. Each time we resplit the deck—when we split the whole deck into two groups, then split each of the two into two more, and so forth—we need to examine all *n* cards.

So Quicksort is an "*n* log *n*" algorithm; for an *n* card deck, it requires roughly *n* log *n* operations if you are lucky. (If you are unlucky, its performance deteriorates, but there are ways to tweak the algorithm to increase your chances of being lucky.) To sort a hundred-card deck, Quicksort needs roughly seven hundred operations, versus ten thousand for insertion sort. To sort a million-card deck, Quicksort needs roughly twenty million operations (versus a trillion). Now let's say you are a computer who can do ten million of these operations in a second. To sort a million-card deck or a million-element list, Quicksort will require roughly two seconds; insertion sort will require on the order of a hundred thousand seconds—roughly a day.

Quicksort *is powerful and simple: a beautiful algorithm.*

The most important tools in computing are programming languages; they are the vehicles, as I have said, for creating virtual machines. To make practical use of an algorithm like Quicksort, you need a programming language. Let's say you are a government agency, your staffers field 6,500 phone complaints an hour, and every evening you want to alphabetize your list of the day's complainers so you can send it over to the IRS and get some audits under way. Quicksort is an excellent way to do the alphabetizing. To write the actual program that is capable of reading the names, sorting them, and filing them away, you need a programming language.

Most working programmers today use one of many languages that are directly descended from Algol 60—the "object of stunning beauty," Alan Perlis called it, the "rounded work of art." Virtually all programmers, whatever language they use, follow practices that were inspired by Algol. The invention of Algol 60 was the most important development in the history of software, and elegance is Algol 60's most important and striking characteristic. It is obsolete today, but its central discoveries live on essentially unchanged in descendent languages like C, C++, Java, Ada, Pascal.

Algol 60 is based on one simple-seeming discovery: big programs can be built out of little programs that are structurally identical to the big ones. This idea is called "recursive structure," *recursive*—an important word in computer science—meaning that you refer to yourself; recursive structures are built of components that are structurally identical to themselves. If an atom were recursive in structure, it would be built out of little atoms instead of protons, neutrons, and electrons. If a car were recursive in structure, the engine, transmission, and so forth would each be little automobiles. Recursive structures, in short, are rare and usually make no sense. But software is a strange material.

Software can be built, the Algol designers observed, in roughly the fashion of an algebraic expression. Tear down a complex algebraic expression—disassemble a multiplication problem, let's say, stipulating that Thing 1 is to be multiplied by Thing 2—and you will find yourself holding a collection of smaller algebraic expressions. Thing 1 is *itself* an algebraic expression, in other words, and Thing 2 likewise. Software can be made to work the same way. It was a brilliantly simple, powerful observation: instead of having to master the rules for many kinds of structure on many scales (instead of having to learn about spark plugs, about the engine that contains the spark plugs, about the powertrain that contains the engine), programmers would need to understand only one set of rules, and those rules would hold good at every scale. Recursive structure brilliantly simplified the synthesis and the analysis of programs, and remains the most important single development in the history of software.

Algol 60 *introduced the seminal idea of recursive structure; the programming-language details and—more important—the ideas it introduced became fundamental to software science and engineering.*

Algol 60 inspired another discovery that was almost as important, in some ways, as recursive structure: the program-building technique called "object-oriented programming," which was first described in 1967 by the designers of the Simula 67 programming language. These designers studied Algol carefully and made an important observation. Algol (like virtually every other language) includes a thing called a "procedure" or "subroutine." If you're building a program and some particular set of steps recurs often, it may be a nuisance to spell out the steps each time; instead, you can bundle them up into a "procedure," and when it comes time to repeat them, write an instruction that says "go do procedure such-and-such, and come back when you're finished."

When an Algol program has been told to execute a procedure, a new "environment" is created automatically, and lives just for the duration of that procedure. This "environment" holds odds and ends that are useful during the execution of the procedure. If you were handling a Senate candidate, you might, by the same token, slip a line into his script saying "now attack your opponent's record on Social Security"—in other words, "go do the Social Security–attack procedure." In the Algol world, as soon as your candidate started the procedure, the right environment would materialize out of thin air—a chart showing how many old people the opponent planned to bump off per year, another emblazoned with incriminating quotes furnished by opposition research, and so forth. As soon as the procedure was complete, its environment would vanish.

The Simula 67 designers made this observation: suppose we let these environments stick around instead of vanishing; in that case, we could build programs in a new way—a program could create lots of little environments, which could then all hang around indefinitely and communicate with one another, like vacationers lounging around the pool sipping coconut sea-slingers with tiny parasol decorations. Needless to say, no one had ever conceived of such a program before, but the Simula 67 designers had all just returned from vacations in Miami—possibly; or possibly the inspiration just came to them. At any rate, each environment would be called an "object," and object-oriented programming was born.

Simula 67 was a language for building simulators—software models of some chunk of the real world—and object-oriented programming was particularly useful for simulator building. If you were simulating a yak stampede, for example, you could create one "object" for each yak in the herd. Each object would track its yak—would record at all times that particular yak's current position, velocity, and so forth. Longer-term yak attributes—fur color, blood type, and any other relevant items—would be recorded in the corresponding object as well. The result is a clean, neat, elegantly structured simulator.

As the Simula designers themselves predicted, object-oriented programming proved to be useful in many areas, not only in simulator building; its popularity grew and use widened when it was taken up by researchers at Xerox, who based a language called Smalltalk on object-orientedness taken to a logical endpoint. Smalltalk was a fascinating and powerful system in its own right, but the key ideas, so far as object-orientedness goes, were all part of Simula 67.

Object-oriented programming was a strikingly elegant discovery not merely for the power it added but because of the way the new power was achieved. It turned up in the attic; Algol 60 had provided the key idea without recognizing it, and all that was necessary in Simula was to grasp the Algol design's significance and add just the smallest, subtlest tweak. Algol had already hit on the idea of a self-contained environment and already provided an environment-creating operation, namely, the procedure call. To achieve object-orientedness, Simula merely needed a second type of procedure call. The original type creates an environment that vanishes when procedure execution is complete; the new type creates an environment that sticks around indefinitely.

Thus Simula was far more powerful, but just barely more complicated, than Algol. The Algol world was a society, say, that knew about stools in the form of wood crates but had yet to invent the table, so you ate your dinner sitting on a stool and cradling a plate (evidently plates had also been invented) in your lap. Simula introduces the revolutionary and profoundly convenient idea of a table, and points out (this is the amazing part) that tables had been latent in society all along. Just stack up a couple of crates and there you are. Reaching a new and deeper understanding of what you already have and thereby achieving something for essentially nothing is the greatest of virtuoso technology accomplishments.

Object-oriented programming *as it emerged in Simula 67 allows software structure to be based on real-world structure, and gives programmers a powerful way to simplify the design and construction of complex programs.*

Computing is a field whose theoretical foundations (such as Turing machines), basic concepts (virtual machines, for example), fundamental algorithms (like Quicksort), and practical tools and methods (for example, the Algol-based programming languages and object-oriented programming) are strikingly beautiful. It is a thing of deep beauty in itself.

But the external shape is what matters to computer users in the end: the form in which computing power is delivered to the user. So we turn now to the beautiful software idea that, if it is neither the deepest of computing's inspirations nor the loveliest, has mattered most in practice: the Apple desktop.

≡FOUR

Rise of the Desktop

What does the world inside your computer look like? Used to be, the appearance of a thing was constrained by the method and materials of its construction. A book's appearance can be adjusted only within narrow boundaries—you can change the cover, vary the dimensions and type font and layout; but chances are, you will still wind up with a stack of pages bound at the edge. The world inside a computer, on the other hand, has no intrinsic appearance. Electronic information is stored in terms of voltage levels, which, strictly speaking, look like nothing. You can give that intracomputer world whatever appearance you like. Computer designers and users reach automatically in this wide sea of possibility for the life raft of traditional, paper-based ways of displaying information. But the computer age is just barely under way, and figuring out what the world inside the computer looks like is the biggest design challenge we have ever faced; we have barely even started.

State of the Art

I have already discussed the Macintosh, but propose to approach it again along a different path. The first time around, the topic was commerce: Given that the Apple desktop is elegant, why is Microsoft beating Apple? The goal this time is to hike the trail that led Apple to its elegant idea. Where did the desktop come from? What are the technical milestones along the way? Which diverging trails do we pass by, and where would they have taken us?

The Macintosh computer and its operating software are hardly the last word on computing elegance. The Macintosh is well over a decade old, and has neither changed nor advanced in any basic way since it was introduced. Its fundamental ideas go back to the 1960s; it's hardly surprising that we can imagine more elegant systems today. (Apple has other problems, aside from stasis. Not long ago, for example, a colleague and I each bought an Apple laptop, two different models, at roughly the same time. Both machines were defective. I'd bought three Macintoshes previously, and one of those was defective also. Statistically my experience proves nothing and has no predictive value, but it is worth mentioning insofar as Apple has a reputation for presuming too far on the loyalty of its devoted customers—and as far as I can tell, deserves it. At the height of the corporate crisis, Apple management put the word out that customers ought to accost strangers seen with competing brands of laptop and upbraid them. Perhaps they'd like some help neatening up around headquarters also? Or maybe we could take the kids for a weekend? Just let us know. After all, what's a customer for?) The Macintosh's basic problem is the earthbound metaphor that underlies it—ideas like "file," "folder," "desktop." These ideas are patterned so closely on preexisting physical models that the software is seriously constrained, can't soar into the cyber-regions computers alone can reach, where paper never went.

The Macintosh does represent two things. First, it is the most elegant solution in general use to the problem of dealing with the world inside the computer; it is more elegant than its predecessors and, on the whole, more elegant than its competitors. Second, it is the most popular solution in general use. The Macintosh itself continues to be a popular machine. And when you add to the Macs in service all desktop machines that run Windows 3.0 or Windows 95 or related systems, you wind up with the world's favorite system by a huge margin.

Where did it come from?

This is a story whose milestones are beautiful technology ideas.

Pre-Macintosh

The first general-purpose electronic digital computer was the ENIAC at the University of Pennsylvania. It used 18,000 vacuum tubes, weighed 30 tons, and filled a large room. Tube computers were gigantic because the tubes themselves took up considerable space, and more space was needed to allow for adequate cooling—tubes run hot.

Elegance Break. The vacuum tube itself was a beautiful invention that revolutionized electronics. The tubes were sometimes referred to as "electric valves," and like any valves they could function as on/off switches; that was their main role in tube computers. But they have broader capabilities. They made the electronics age possible because they can amplify weak electric signals. And the electronics revolution hinged, of course, on weak signals that needed amplifying—radio signals pulled out of space, phone signals at the end of long wires, microphone signals that mimic the shapes of sound waves.

A vacuum tube has a filament (as in a lightbulb) at its

center; when current runs through it, the filament heats up and throws off electrons. A wire grid surrounds the filament, and a metal plate wraps around the grid. Thrown-off electrons travel through the grid to the plate, but depending on grid voltage it can be easy or hard for them to get through. This flow of electrons from filament to plate constitutes a relatively strong electric signal that can be modulated by a weak signal on the grid; let your tube heat up, put your weak signal on the grid, and an amplified signal, faithfully reflecting the original's shape, emerges from the plate. If the amplified signal isn't strong enough, merely feed it to the grid on another tube.

On a typical early computer, a tube blew somewhere and needed to be replaced several times an hour. How did we get from there to here? From those room-sized multimillion-dollar models to the machine you buy at Sears? Personal computing had been predicted for a long time, but the form in which it emerged was a surprise.

Putting technology in the hands of the individual is the American way: while the Europeans perfected public transportation, Americans (influenced, of course, by our much more diffuse settlement patterns) bought cars. In the late 1940s and early 1950s TVs were rare, and often deployed in public gathering spots; in the early '50s high-fidelity sound was another rarity, and college students organized "listening rooms" where you could hear classical recordings in hi-fi. Shared telephones were common in some places throughout the 1950s. But no one doubted that in time virtually every family would have a personal telephone.

It was inevitable that "personal" computers would come to mind. Compared to cars, TVs, stereos, or telephones, however, personal computers posed an obvious problem: What would you *do* with one? By the mid-1960s computers were a prominent, ubiquitous part of the American scene. The "IBM card" was a joke—the cards that came into the public's hands often carried the pompous little message "Do not fold, spindle, or mutilate." The public duly obeyed, and snickered. Computers did the payrolls and handled billing at large companies, and had various obscure scientific uses that the public respected but did not understand. They seemed about as essential to the average happy home as a Saturn booster rocket or an atomic pastrami slicer.

This point is important, because there is a remarkable fact about computers that is so fundamental to their story we barely notice it, yet it matters profoundly to their history, their status today, and their likely future. The drive to create personal computers and bring them to every family in the country was *not* motivated by anything in particular that people wanted to do with computers. The automobile industry came about because cars were a good way to get around, and telephones were obviously a good way to communicate. But computers weren't a good way to do anything that private citizens particularly needed to do. Personal computers arose from the conviction that computers were just *good*, period.

The computer is invented first. Uses for the computer come afterward. The "killer app" phenomenon is basic to computer history; the term refers to an "application," or piece of software, that is so useful, people buy the computer in order to run the application. On the first widely used personal computer, for example—the Apple II—the killer app was Visicalc, the first spreadsheet program. New machines are developed and released for no reason other than the fact that they are better on technical grounds than the old ones. The applications, it is assumed, will materialize somehow; and they always do. As recently as 1977, the president of Digital Equipment Corporation—then a computer industry powerhouse and still a very big company—announced that "there is no reason for any individual to have a computer in their home"; and if the citation is accurate, he was right, at least insofar as he was implicitly forecasting the collapse of grammar.

But most experts assumed that if the computers were there, something would turn up for them to do. By the late 1960s, many were convinced that computing was coming to your home the way electricity did: it would be generated at a central plant and pumped in over wires. Although this idea lost out to the personal computer on the desktop, it had undeniable elegance and is likely to return one day—although in a radically different shape from what people anticipated.

The power-plant idea arose because of time sharing, which had been invented in the early 1960s. It was the first beautiful idea in the history of operating systems: a way of programming a computer that allowed many people to use one machine simultaneously. It was such a dazzling trick that many of the users who benefited from it never did understand it. You could take one big computer and attach, say, one hundred terminals to it. (At first a "terminal" meant a teletype; it came in time to refer to a display screen and a keyboard.) A hundred people could sit down at the terminals and all type instructions to the computer simultaneously. The computer would turn its attention from one terminal to the next so rapidly, doing a bit of work for one user and then storming on to the next one, that all hundred people would have the impression that they were getting the machine's undivided attention.

Time sharing transcends the limitations of only one computer and many computer users by making one computer seem to be many.

A typical 1960s mainframe was enormously less powerful than today's garden-variety personal computer. How could it have kept one hundred adults satisfied? Because they were far more easily satisfied, computationally speaking, than today's average six-year-old. There were no fancy images to generate, no fancy anything. Computers mainly did sorting and filing and database chores, and numerical calculations.

The existence of time sharing suggested to computer scientists that, eventually, everyone would have a terminal at home. The hundred thousand residents of a small city would all draw computing power from a central computing plant, where each of a handful of powerful computers would juggle thousands of users simultaneously. You would be billed monthly for "connect time." The idea of the computer power plant inspired a mammoth research project of the late 1960s called Multics, an operating system built by Bell Labs, General Electric (then a major computer producer), and MIT (reportedly a university in Massachusetts). It was enormously complicated and conceived in rings, like Dante's hell. At the blazing core was the huge computer itself, the GE–645—a machine with less computing power in its entire mammoth room-filling awesomeness than a broken-down jalopy PC. As you journeyed from the inner rings outward, you would travel through software zones of decreasing "privilege"—inner-ring programs were allowed to control the computer directly; the users, far out on the rim, were strictly limited in the commands they were allowed to execute and, consequently, the damage they had it in their power to wreak.

Multics was the ultimate system for an era in which a powerful computer was a very big, complicated, imposing machine. It is a shame, in a way, that the age of the gigantic mainframe is over, because those installations were gripping entertainment in a way today's bland boxes can never be. The "machine room" of those years was a place like no other. Often it was glassed-in and you could watch from the outside, which added to its aura of power and dynamism.

The mainframe turns out to have been a freakish anomaly. It was as if, for a couple of decades, the world had been inhabited by a race of towering "visible men" with organs in plain view behind their see-through plastic shells. Human beings are fantastically complex machines, but we rarely think of them as such because the mechanism is mainly hidden, and most of the action takes place at a scale too small to be seen. Likewise with a modern desktop computer. But inside a classic machine room of the 1960s, the central processor had a large floor-standing box to itself, of the size and shape of a decent-size refrigerator, and there were many other large cabinets full of memory. A modern disk drive is far smaller than a shoebox and mounted inside the main desktop cabinet, but a '60s disk drive stood on the floor and came up to your waist; the whirling stacks of metal platters inside made it shudder and tremble like a priestess of Delphi about to disclose an oracle. The huge reels of the magnetic tape drives spun with improbable split-second precision, moving instantaneously from stopped to spinning and back again. Operators rushed around grabbing output from the line printers, mounting tapes, squinting at the cryptic display on the console, and acting important; it was one of the strangest landscapes that has ever been created, and utterly intriguing. A child could gaze at it for hours.

Though Multics was used at only a handful of sites, it introduced many ideas that became important later on, and inspired—in the sense in which the First World War inspired the League of Nations—a follow-up effort that yielded one of the most widely used and important operating systems in the world. A couple of scientists at Bell Labs were so irritated by the monumental complexity of Multics that they built a system called Unics (later Unix) and, just to get even, made it as simple as possible.

Unix is beautiful in some ways, and was a prodigy of simple power at the time. Dennis Ritchie and Ken Thompson designed it; they hoped that users would judge "the most important characteristics of the system" to be "simplicity, elegance and ease of use."

Unix *should* be a hero of elegance, but the system as it exists today has a split personality. It was intended from the start for sophisticated users, software developers; it had to be flexible and powerful. Sometimes it achieved power by means of simple, brilliant design and sometimes by means of complexity so exquisitely rococo it made you turn green and reach for the airsickness bag. And the system has grown over the years like a one-way trailer park. New features arrive but old ones don't depart, and the relaxed ambiance means that newcomers aren't held, necessarily, to high aesthetic standards.

The "pipe" feature of the Unix shell (the "shell" being itself one of Unix's most important inventions—a go-between program that presents the operating system with user requests) is a classic demonstration of power through simplicity. It allows you to glue prefabricated programs together into a "pipeline"—the first program's output becomes the second's input. For example: if you are running many programs and you want to find out whether some particular one is active, you can pipe together an active-program-lister and a name-searcher. The first program pumps a list of all active programs into the second, which searches for the name you want and notifies you if it scores a hit.

Suppose, on the other hand, that you suspect you have put a file somewhere but don't remember where it is. Unix has a hierarchical directory structure—a directory can contain files and other directories, which may contain other directories in turn, to whatever depth you like. Unix originated hierarchical directories in the modern sense; today virtually all operating systems have them. Your task, then, is to search through all your directories for the file named "alonzo." You're in luck: Unix systems have a command called "find" that is intended for exactly that purpose. It comes in twenty-four *basic* flavors that can be combined in many, many ways. Here is the first example from Unix on-line documentation:

find $HOME \(-name a.out -o -name "*.o' \) – atime +7 - exec rm [lftbr][rtbr] \;

These commands don't merely find your files; they perform various other operations, too. In fact, it is a sure bet that, if you played your cards right, you could get *find* to print out the complete lyrics of *Oklahoma!* in Albanian, and certain versions were capable of displaying a neat proof of Fermat's last theorem also, but unfortunately no one could ever figure out how to make them do it. In short, *find* is powerful but not simple. It is the farthest thing from simple.

It was assumed, at any rate, that home computing would arrive in the form of terminals connected to a central plant. But in the 1970s matters took an unexpected turn.

The technology of integrated circuits made it possible to pack electronic components into ever smaller packages, and suddenly it seemed possible that the future of personal computers would be less like electric power and more like toasters. By the mid-1950s, integrated-circuit pioneers at Bell Labs had figured out how to fit four transistors on a silicon chip. By the early '70s, the technology had come far enough to make handheld electronic calculators possible. (I first saw one as a college freshman at a chemistry lecture in the fall of 1972. The professor held one up triumphantly: "this little baby," I remember him saying, had cost him four hundred-odd dollars; but someday, electronic calculators like his would make slide rules obsolete. We were impressed, and strained to get a look.) By 1975 a personal computer was available, powered by a chip called the Intel 8080—a chip from which today's Intel processors, which drive the IBM PC and all its loyal clones, are directly descended.

This machine, usually judged to have been the first personal computer, was the Altair 8800. It cost $387 and you had to assemble it yourself. It had no keyboard, monitor, or software; it was just a slab of pure computer, medium rare. You programmed the Altair by putting binary numbers (strings of 1's and 0's) directly into memory by means of switches on the front panel. Output was in binary also, via front-panel lights. *There* was a man's computer designed by men for men!

But the emergence of the personal computer is a more complicated affair than Intel to Altair to Apple. A 1969 publicity photo shows a kitchen equipped with a tasteful Honeywell minicomputer deployed like a cooking island. Vegetables rest in a basket on top. The computer sold for $10,600 net of vegetables, and what a housewife would do with one in her kitchen was no clearer then than it is today. Perhaps design an atom bomb to drop on someone at Honeywell. The Honeywell machine ushered in no technology revolutions, but reminds us that minicomputers were crucial in the evolution of today's computer world.

To fool around with computers in high school during the early 1970s, I worked at a teletype connected via phone line to a central time-shared machine; but when I learned to program for real as a college student, the machine I worked on was a PDP–8 minicomputer built by the Digital Equipment Corporation. It was 1975, and the PDP–8 was itself a personal computer of sorts—a box roughly a yard wide by a yard deep and a foot high. It was designed for mounting in a laboratory rack, and was used mainly by scientists to control complex laboratory setups. (I encountered it in a physics course, intended to equip you with enough digital electronics to run your future laboratory.) The 8 was a lovable machine, not powerful enough to qualify as elegant but abundantly simple and beautifully designed. Its upmarket brother, the PDP–11, was a beautiful machine indeed.

Progress is faster by far in hardware than software, but software discoveries are longer lasting. The important ones transcend hardware. The object-oriented software techniques invented in 1967 remain important; the only place you will find a 1967 computer today is in a museum or antiques shop. But, of course, brilliant and inspiring hardware designs exist, obsolete or no, and the PDP–11 was one.

Was the Altair or one of the DEC minicomputers the first personal computer? Neither. The *real* progenitor of today's desktop machines was a remarkable computer invented by scientists at the Xerox Palo Alto Research Lab in the mid-

1970s, called the Alto. The first Alto was assembled in 1973; it initiated the elegance revolution that led directly to the Macintosh, Windows, and today's computer world.

Elegance break. At the New York World's Fair of 1964–65, IBM's pavilion presented a future-of-computing very different from the one that happened; it did so using the dead language of modernism amid the long-dead culture of mid-1940s through mid-1960s America. It is worth a look nonetheless because it was elegant and interesting. It was a public versus private view of computing; IBM machines weren't the sort of things a person could own. "IBM knows very well it can't sell or rent a computer to me," a *Holiday* magazine writer announced apropos of the IBM pavilion, "and most likely not to you either." So the IBM exhibit was a sort of park focused on computation the way some other park might center on a waterfall or a beautiful stretch of coast; computing was an edifying, entertaining, exotic force of nature.

The pavilion was designed by Eero Saarinen, whose office specialized in the swoopily dramatic. It was a huge movie theater–containing egg, supported several stories above the ground on an elaborate steel framework like a stylized forest. To get into the egg, you sat in a wall of bleacher seats that glided upward—a gangplank tugged smoothly into Noah's ark from the inside. Once aboard, you saw a nine-screen presentation about computers and brains conceived by Charles Eames, the distinguished designer of furniture and other things.

After you saw the show, you could wander around under the canopy, where manifestations of computing bubbled to the surface like hot springs at a spa. You could name any date in the last hundred years, for example, an attractive young lady would enter your date into a computer, and a newspaper headline from that very date would emerge, to be displayed in lights on a message board and printed on a card you could take home. Other exhibits illustrated principles of mathematical logic and probability that underlie the science of computation.

It was one of the big hits of the '64 Fair, which itself marked the end of an era. In the late 1960s American confidence and exuberance sank into dust with the heartbreaking majesty of a dynamited skyscraper. That is another story, but our culture is still haunted by the interrupted trajectory, by the journey we abruptly broke off so we could head off on a different one. The IBM pavilion is a landmark by the abandoned roadside. It was a swaggering culture, the one we abandoned, so sleek and self-confident it could get on your nerves, but we often forget how playful it could be also, and how elegant. We think of modernism as the dead style of the heartless office slab, but modernism was, also, the gigantic egg that you slipped into on a gliding bleacher. At its best it was the wittiest, cleverest, and most democratic style in history, and the IBM egg with its forgotten computers and forgotten view of computing was modernism's worthy representative. No book has ever captured the essence of that remarkable culture, but when some book finally does, the IBM pavilion is likely to put in an appearance.

Xerox

In 1969, Xerox Corporation decided to set up a research lab for computing and information. The Xerox Palo Alto Research Center opened in 1970; for the next decade, ideas emanating from PARC (as the center was called) dominated software research. During the decade after that, they infiltrated the world at large. The corporate powers at Xerox itself never understood or capitalized on PARC's inventions, but give them this: during the 1970s, they assembled a spectacular group of researchers, gave them money and facilities, and allowed them to work in peace. Whatever its motives, Xerox made a gigantic contribution to the science and practice of computing and deserves our gratitude. No American corporation would even *think* of underwriting such a venture today. Were an executive even to mumble such an idea in a distracted whisper while at home in bed having a bad dream, he would be shot at dawn.

I gave a couple of talks at PARC as a new researcher in the mid-1980s, well after the glory days; early one morning I found myself alone outside in a vine-decorated plaza full of honeysuckle fragrance. You experienced, standing outside PARC, the essence of California culture at its best: its beckoning exotic air. Its "step into my inner courtyard" murmur. Palo Alto is dominated most of the year by gentle hills slowly frying, and parking lots where the sun glare is sharp as glass and the view hurts. The PARC building itself is concrete and could pass for a fancy pillbox. But inner courtyards are irresistible, with their promise of flowers or trickling fountains or exotic ideas behind the walls; the offer is forever alluring. PARC in the mid-'80s still had an aura of inventiveness, freethinking, and fresh ideas.

PARC launched its computing operations by building a large time-shared computer. But in 1972, Butler Lampson, Chuck Thatcher, and Edward McCreight set to work on a different kind of machine. Also part of the project was Alan Kay, who was interested (and still is) in computers that were simple enough for children to use. Kay's obsession with children is a central theme in the triumph that follows. In coming years the hardware builders found themselves able to assemble ever more powerful machines—and Kay, meanwhile, insisted that the operating system be kept simple.

The first Alto was completed on April 1, 1973: a personal computer for the use of PARC researchers. The Alto came in a box on casters roughly a yard on a side. It was designed to slip under a table. The mouse, keyboard, and screen sat on the tabletop; the screen was an upright rectangle, a shape called "portrait style" today—like a large sheet of typing paper standing at attention.

The Alto played a central role in the rise of the window. Windows are a crucial piece of computing elegance because they liberate your channel of communication with the computer from the exigencies of a particular chunk of hardware. Without windows, the size of your screen limits your communication channel: human and machine communicate through a single rectangular chink in a blank wall. But once you have windows, you have as many separate channels to the computer as you want.

Windows were first developed by Ivan Sutherland when he was a graduate student at MIT in the early 1960s. He built a program called Sketchpad, which is the forerunner of all computer-based drawing and design tools; using Sketchpad you could make drawings on a screen with a lightpen, and the computer could adjust, clean up, and manipulate them.

Late in the 1960s Douglas Engelbart built another system around windows. Like Sutherland's, Engelbart's windows were created by dividing the screen into smaller rectangles by means of straight lines. Windows never overlapped. Alan Kay took the idea a crucial step further when he invented overlapping windows at Xerox. "All of us thought the Alto display was incredibly small," he explained later—"all of us" being his colleagues at PARC; "and it's clear you've got to have overlapping windows if you don't have a large display." Obvious? Certainly, in retrospect.

It might sound like a minor tweak to the original idea— but if every window must be wholly visible, you are still limited by the size of the screen. If windows can overlap, you can create a pile of nearly unlimited or (if you allow some to be hidden entirely) actually unlimited size. By the end of 1973, overlapping windows had arrived on the Alto.

The Window: a milestone in the effort to liberate computing from computers. A computer is just one machine, a screen is a single plot of real estate, but windows allow you to create as many communication channels as you choose between yourself and your running programs.

The Alto had another revolutionary feature that complemented Kay's windows, a *bit-mapped display*. Until the Alto—and long after, in conventional circles—a computer screen had been a machine for displaying lines of characters. Each screen had certain characters it knew how to display—typically the digits, upper- and lowercase letters, and some punctuation marks and arithmetic symbols. A certain number of lines would fit on the screen, and the computer's job was to tell the screen which characters to put on which lines. It used a numerical code (the most common was called ASCII) to specify characters: "On line one, give me characters 60, 61, 73 . . . ," and so on, for each line on the screen.

The Alto's bit-mapped screen worked differently. It was a grid of pixels, each pixel being one dot on the screen; the computer's job was to specify exactly what the screen should do about every single pixel. On a black-and-white screen each pixel had exactly two options. If the computer wanted the letter A to appear at the upper-left corner, it couldn't merely call out the code; assuming the background was white, it needed to tell the screen to switch a certain group of pixels from white to black—a group that, collectively, formed the letter A.

The programmer has a far more complicated job in the bit-mapped world, and the computer assumes a heavier burden too–it needs to set aside enough memory to store an image of the entire screen, and needs also to be able to move that information out of memory and into the screen rapidly. The whole system executes a kind of transition broadly resembling what would happen if an expert typist had to throw out his machine and learn calligraphy. Operations once taken for granted—display an A—now have to be carried out in detail. But the gain in flexibility is enormous. A bit-mapped screen can display lines of text as well as the old-fashioned screen, but can do so in as many fonts and sizes as the programmer cares to create, and throw in as many special symbols as he wants; it can also show drawings and images of all kinds and display overlapping windows.

One final crucial part of the Alto story, a gadget that wasn't part of the original package, was acquired soon after: the mouse. Engelbart invented it; his mouse had three buttons and was intended, unlike modern ones, to be moved with the right hand as you manipulated a special five-key keyboard with your left. It looked like a brick. Larry Tesler (later of PARC) saw Engelbart's mouse in 1966. He didn't like it: "I thought cursor keys were much better," he said. So at PARC,

we literally took people off the streets who had never seen a computer. In three or four minutes they were happily editing away, using the cursor keys. At that point I was going to show them the mouse and prove they could select text faster than with the cursor keys. Then I was going to show them that they didn't like it.

It backfired. I would have them spend an hour working the cursor keys, which got them really used to the keys. Then I would teach them about the mouse. They would say, "That's interesting but I don't think I need it." Then they would play with it a bit, and after two minutes they never touched the cursor keys again.

The mark of an important invention—almost the *definition* of an important invention—is that it turns out to be useful for reasons beyond what the inventors originally intended. "We were surprised time and again," says Bob Taylor, who was head of PARC in the glory days, "by applications of the time-sharing system that nobody planned but someone invented anyway." The instance he mentions was users' needing to share files—which led to the invention of electronic mail. The mouse became a crucial piece of a computing environment that didn't exist when the mouse itself was invented.

The Alto was impressive, but Xerox was not impressed. It never marketed the Alto, and by the early 1980s most of the researchers who developed it had packed up and left. Historians today tend to read corporate Xerox's response to the Alto as a disastrous failure of imagination—which it clearly was, to a point. It brings to mind the story of Fred Astaire's first screen test at Paramount; the executive who turned him down is supposed to have reported: "Can't act. Can't sing. Balding. Can dance a little."

But in a deeper sense, corporate Xerox's instincts were right—the desktop idea did indeed face tough going in the market for years—and constitute another demonstration of the beauty paradox at work. Before the desktop interface broke into the mainstream it was rejected twice, by the majority of corporate buyers in the 1980s and by Xerox executives in the 1970s. Both rejections have logical explanations and each is tinged with looniness. Corporate buyers rejected the Macintosh in the 1980s, although businesses are supposed to be especially interested in ease of use and low maintenance costs. Xerox executives rejected the desktop in the 1970s, but why did they create the Palo Alto Reseach Lab in the first place? The stated goal as of 1969 was for Xerox to become "the architect of information"; how could any lab have hit a more perfect bull's-eye? It can't be that Xerox executives were against newness on principle—if so, why set up a research lab? Is prejudice against beautiful technology a deep-lying part of our national character?

The Emergence of Apple

The Apple Computer Company had reached an agreement with Xerox whereby a small Apple delegation would be shown PARC's discoveries. Steven Jobs may be no inventor, but to his credit he recognized elegance when he saw it and understood its significance. That is more than Xerox's top executives can say, or the thousands of computer cognoscenti whose first reaction to the Macintosh was a shrug.

Apple had hit it big with a 1977 computer called the Apple II. Stephen Wozniak was a young engineer at Hewlett-Packard when he designed a computer kit similar to the Altair 8800, but capable of having a keyboard and monitor attached. Hewlett-Packard wasn't interested in his invention, so he and friend Jobs set up shop and marketed the kit as the Apple Computer. It sold for $666.66. The follow-up Apple II came fully assembled and went for $1,195. Wozniak is widely acknowledged to have been a maker of beautiful machines. Fellow technologists regarded his "virtuoso design" for the Apple II's main circuit board, Steven Levy writes, as "a beautiful work of art."

Apple made lots of money on the Apple II, assisted by its killer app Visicalc, which introduced the idea of a software spreadsheet—a sophisticated calculator capable of tracking and displaying many related computations simultaneously.

Apple planned to follow up its Apple II success with a radically different type of computer named the Lisa—a more powerful and sophisticated machine. IBM had moved into the personal computer market, and the PC was a big hit in the business world. Apple's characteristically modest plan for the Lisa was to gallop straight into the heart of the business market, guns blazing, and take over.

The Lisa was intended from the beginning to have a bit-mapped, "paper-look" screen: characters were to be displayed black-on-white, versus the white- (or green- or, my personal favorite, orange-) on-black you would find on old-fashioned conventional displays. When Jobs and company saw the Alto, however, their plans for the Lisa expanded dramatically. The new machine took on windows and a mouse and icons, but not quite in the same way the Alto had them. When you observe that Microsoft borrowed all the significant ideas in Windows from Apple, you are sometimes informed in response that Apple, after all, borrowed them all from Xerox; but that's not quite true. Apple borrowed a great deal but made important improvements, too. The Alto relied on menus as ever-present middlemen between user and machine: to move or resize a window, you indicated *which* window with the mouse, but relied on a menu to specify that you wanted to *move* the window. On the Lisa you could do the operation directly, with no intervening menu.

On the Lisa you could also, for the first time, create a new window and run a program inside merely by double-clicking on the program's icon. The Lisa introduced double-clicking, too; Xerox's mouse and Engelbart's had had three buttons, but Apple brought the button count down to one and compensated by adding new ways to click. Lisa introduced the "menu bar," a row of words across the top of the screen that, when you point and click at them, cause menus to appear. Every application program uses the menu bar in approximately the same way, which is a help in getting used to new software. These improvements and others went into the Macintosh as well, which was intended to be an even more sophisticated machine but, unlike the Lisa, a not-too-expensive one.

Compared to the PCs of the time and their Microsoft operating systems, the Macintosh looks in retrospect like an obvious breakthrough: simpler and more powerful, hence more elegant by far. Steven Levy gives one example: to call up a file on the PC under Microsoft's DOS, you had to type the file's name in full; on the Mac, you merely pointed with the mouse to an icon representing the file you wanted. For most people pointing is quicker than typing, and there is another important gain, too: a typing error on the PC would lead to the wrong file being summoned or an unwanted new one created. "If you mistyped a single character of the file (as I often did)," Levy writes, the system would assume you were not opening a previous file, but beginning a brand-new file with the typo as its title. And you would sit there, frozen, for twenty seconds that seemed eternal, as the computer went through its paces so you could then delete that unwanted file and try once more to get the file you desired.

Or, in my case, you would charge angrily onward and not bother to delete the typo file, and your disk would fill up with garbage.

You can almost hear the "computer boxes are—computer boxes" crowd: "*Twenty seconds??* So you *wait* twenty seconds. Big deal. 'Elegance' is important because it saves you *twenty seconds?*" Yes, elegance is important because it saves you twenty seconds—repeatedly. The difference between software that leaves you in peace and software that constantly takes little nips out of your thought processes—twenty seconds here, twenty there—is the difference between a pleasantly productive environment and an irritatingly unproductive one. The seconds add up, and the sheer fact of interruption is more important still.

Windows made it easy to shift contexts from one program to another; the bit-mapped screen enormously widened the machine's graphic range; the standard application interface made it easy to get acquainted with new programs.

The Macintosh's shortcomings were serious (the early models were slow and had too little memory), but there was nothing subtle about its advantages. Its advantages—and this was the whole point—weren't esoteric or technical; they were obvious to anyone who had ever used a computer. And yet when the Macintosh was introduced, loads of people succeeded in being unimpressed.

Late in 1986 the *New York Times* summarized popular wisdom about the Macintosh: people dislike it for being "too slow, having little software, not being expandable by the addition of specialized circuit boards, and being incompatible with the I.B.M. computers that dominate corporate desk-tops." But the machine *was* starting to catch on because it was being used "for so-called desktop publishing, the layout and printing of newsletters, brochures and other documents."

This is a text worth pondering. The Macintosh was bad for specific technical and business reasons, and on the other hand it was good for specific technical and business reasons. Between the lines, the *Times* is faithfully reporting the hinge of this story: elegance was the Mac's outstanding characteristic—"a lot of people bought the Mac," recall the software executive saying in 1986, "because it was so amazing"; but in the final analysis, when you took a *serious* look at the marketplace, elegance was neither here nor there. It didn't count, analysts believed, when people bypassed the Macintosh, and didn't count when people bought it.

In time viewpoints changed, and elegance was recognized as the Macintosh's key accomplishment. In his 1996 book *The Road Ahead*, Bill Gates writes that he believed as of 1983 that "future interfaces would be graphical" and that Microsoft had to "set a new standard in which pictures and fonts (typefaces) would be part of an easier-to-use interface." But the inevitability of Mac-style graphical interfaces was by no means obvious at the time.

A month after the Mac was first released, one computer magazine article mobilized all the exuberant enthusiasm at its command to pronounce it "rather impressive." "I hate the mouse. I hate the icons. I hate the hype. I hate the one-size-fits-all operating environment and philosophy"—a 1988 piece in *Government Computer News*. "The Macintosh's operating system is friendly," a 1984 article reported, "but at what price?" It was fine for the novice, the article said, "but users are novices only once." "The jury is still out," according to a 1986 article in a professional engineers' magazine, "on whether the 'Macintosh interface' is the best way for humans to interact with computers. Experienced users, in particular, express the need for an alternative." "The jury is still definitely out," said a 1989 article, apropos of whether icons are as useful as they are cracked up to be. Once the Macintosh was introduced, the jury, as you can see, excused itself and stayed out for the rest of the decade. In 1989 there remained, one writer claimed, a "still-deep-seated aversion to mouse use in the DOS world."

Some part of consumer resistance to elegance merely reflects people's healthy disinclination to change their working methods when they are managing all right as things stand. And the inventors of elegant technologies do have a tendency to wrap them in hyperbole, like nervous mothers outfitting their children in thirteen sweaters against a chilly day. Engelbart believed that the discoveries of his "augmentation research center" would lead to "changes in our ways of thinking and working" that were likely to be "more pervasive and extreme than ANY OF US appreciates—a revolution like the development of writing and the printing press lumped together." Yet the hype is indispensable. If creative people didn't have serenely powerful egos, how would they withstand the terrific pressures that are brought to bear in the scientific and technical communities, and the intelligentsia generally, to conform?

In the end, the desktop's inventors were, of course, largely right and the rest of the world largely wrong—until, at long last, the thing caught on. The inventors knew they had a beautiful item on their hands, and beauty wins in the end.

FIVE

Beyond the Desktop

For many people, the desktop represents a permanent, perpetually valid contribution to computer interface design. "Like many other brilliant ideas," Steven Levy writes of the desktop model as it emerged from PARC, "once introduced it is unimaginable to conceive of working without it." The desktop might indeed be a semipermanent part of the computer landscape, if we define it broadly enough—windows in some form, for example, are unlikely to disappear anytime soon. But many other aspects of the model are bound to be supplanted before long. That will happen not because of the desktop's weaknesses but because of some other system's strengths; not, in other words, as a result of any systematic analysis of today's software but because someone had a brainstorm and the result was a new and different interface.

I will describe here one such "candidate system"—a computer interface that is different from the desktop and is also, according to some people (as always, the judgment is subjective), more elegant. But there are reasons to disbelieve in the

87

desktop's permanent preeminence that have nothing to do with this proposed new system, that emerge from a systematic consideration of the desktop's own strengths and weaknesses. Such an analysis doesn't tell us where to go, and can't in itself affect the desktop's popularity, but is useful preparation for evaluating new systems. It comes in three sections: the desktop's limitations compared to the physical model that inspired it; the limitations imposed by "paradigm drag"; and the new and unexplored possibilities created by the Internet.

It happens that the imminent demise of the desktop is a favorite industry theme nowadays; several major companies have announced that they will be abandoning it in favor of something or other to do with the Web. Your desktop will be replaced, they say, by your Website—a Website being, of course, a set of screen displays and associated files and software that can be reached from afar over the Internet. But in itself, "replacing the desktop with the Website" means nothing. The desktop is a sophisticated information-organizing strategy; the Website is not. To claim that the desktop is obsolete and ought to be replaced by the Website is like claiming that your library's shelving scheme is obsolete, so the books ought to be yanked out and dumped on the floor. It's worth keeping in mind also that, although it is useful and fun to be able to reach millions of information treasure troves over the Internet, no serious person's on-line life is or ever will be centered on Websites in today's sense. What matters 90-plus percent of the time is *your own* files and mail and calendar and data, not the rest of the world's. If we throw out the desktop, our first duty is to make sure that we provide an organizing strategy for a person's own stash of data that works well as a replacement.

Tying the Macintosh display to the idea of a desktop was a brilliant move. The mark of a well-designed interface is that, as soon as you see it, you immediately form guesses about how it works, and the guesses turn out basically right. The desktop metaphor was brilliant because it gave people a basis for making basically correct guesses about how the computer worked. Manipulating a physical file of information entails moving it around, so it makes sense that you manipulate the electronic version by moving its icon around the screen. It makes sense that you can place it on the desktop or throw it out by moving the icon around in the proper way. People are accustomed to arranging sheets of paper on their actual desktops in such a way that objects of immediate attention are on top, fully visible, and others that will be needed soon are near the top—perhaps partly visible. Managing windows entails basically the same sort of arranging.

On the other hand, the physical analogy on which the Macintosh operating system is based also creates a problem we might call "paradigm drag." Kay himself refers to exactly this issue when he writes, about folders, that "one of his longstanding pet hates" is to have them "behave anything like their physical counterparts." The electronic desktop inevitably lacks certain good properties that all physical desktops have. It counters with advantages that physical desktops lack; but the drag effect comes in when the electronic version is cramped by the limitations of the physical one. No physical desktop can do something or other, and as a result it doesn't occur to software designers to give that property to the electronic version, either. Basing software on a familiar physical system is a strategy that cuts both ways.

For example: you can take a paper file wherever you want, but to use a computer file you need a computer. Portable computers are easy to carry around, but it's likely to be quite a while before you can stuff one in your briefcase or coat pocket as nonchalantly as you can a sheaf of papers. Forget about paper's weight and flexibility advantages; the mere fact that computers are relatively delicate and expensive imposes costs in time and effort when you move one around. You can work with papers when you are sprawled on a sofa, sitting on a beach, riding a subway, having coffee at a lunch counter, lying in bed unable to sleep at three in the morning, meeting with a dozen colleagues at a conference table and ostensibly examining the budget report you are holding in your lap, with your customary grave attention to all the little details. Yes, you *could* use a portable computer in all these circumstances, but it's a pain and few people do. Computerized files inevitably give something up to paper ones in portability, and that is likely to remain true for some time.

Given a collection of old-fashioned files, each holding a bunch of papers, you can judge a file's size and maybe contents by its look and heft. You can look for the big file, the file with crayon scribbling on the folder, the file with overhead-projector slides spilling out. Computerized files don't ordinarily give you visual or tactile cues.

You can, as I have noted, take papers off your desk and carry them wherever you want; you can also scoop up a bunch, dump them in a drawer, and retrieve them later—or dump them on a different desk back home, even a desk made by an entirely different manufacturer with radically different ideas about desk design.

The relevant comparison here is between a paper document and a window on your computer screen; each window, recall, is an electronic document on your electronic desktop. The windows on a computer screen are stuck there. Using today's conventional software you can't scoop a bunch of windows off your screen and stash them wholly out of sight and out of the way. You can't ordinarily move a window from one computer to another. You need to move the file (which may entail copying it onto a diskette first), then recreate the window on the new computer.

In the world of paper, you name documents only when you want to. It's natural for an article or book or poem to have a title, so you give them titles. When you write a letter, on the other hand, it would be unnatural and pointless to bestow a name on it. The same holds for memos, reminder notes, drafts, back-of-the-envelope calculations, sketches, shopping lists, and all sorts of other informal documents. But in the electronic world, today's conventional operating systems force you to give every document a name, which is a nuisance and a waste of time. They force you to file it in a folder or directory, which is likewise a nuisance and a waste of time.

A desk is a lot bigger than a computer screen—and if it's not big enough, you always have the floor or the dining room table. Computer windows can't be spread out on the floor.

To make up for these limitations, the computer must offer compensating advantages, and of course it does. But the paradigm drag created by the desktop model hems it in.

For example: a paper file has to stay put until someone moves it, but the electronic version can be moved automatically; an electronic file can be stored under warehouse conditions (in a place where it may not be directly accessible) dirt-cheaply. These facts suggest that old or unpopular electronic files ought to be warehoused automatically, and retrieved automatically when you need them. Software, in other words, ought to monitor your use of files and the space remaining on your computer in which to store them. When space gets tight, it ought to remove files automatically and drop them in a warehouse somewhere.

This warehousing might take place by means of a network connection, but could also work on a stand-alone computer. When space got tight on your disk, the operating system would send you a message—"I want to move some files out to diskette; please pop in a diskette when you have a chance, and mark it 31493qxx." When you tried to open a file that had been archived, you'd get the inverse message: "if you would please pop in the diskette labelled 31493qxx, I'll get that file back for you." But automatic warehousing hasn't emerged as a part of today's standard electronic desktop. Automatic warehousing doesn't exist and would never work in the physical-desktop world (there are commercial paper-warehousing operations, but they don't specialize in split-second service); so it's not surprising that it hasn't emerged as part of the electronic-desktop worldview, either.

Warehousing is one part of a broader issue. Among "knowledge workers," much time is still devoted to managing paper: organizing, classifying, filing, retrieving. Suppose you were given the opportunity to conduct your life in an environment that was completely paper-free, except for any papers you might need right at the moment. Some "paper-management company" has the magical ability to accept and stash for safekeeping any document you are through with—you simply hand it to an employee posted discreetly at all times beside your desk. The company can produce any filed document you need instantaneously; you describe the document in a straightforward, natural way ("Get me the Zeppelin report" or "my last phone bill" or "the letter from whomever about the warranty on my mandolin"). The right document materializes immediately, having been conveyed from the central warehouse by turbo-rocket platform.

This service is available, let's say, for a small monthly fee. Some people aren't interested; they have no trouble handling their own paper. But many others are likely to find the company's offer attractive. Once you sign up, after all, you no longer spend any time organizing, classifying, searching, or retrieving. You no longer worry about documents misplaced, buried, or accidentally thrown out. You no longer need any desk drawers or file cabinets; you merely rent exactly as much space as you need inside someone else's file cabinets—and whether the cabinets are big enough, secure enough, and fireproof enough is someone else's worry; the company guarantees that your documents will be safe. Your physical whereabouts no longer matter to your work plans, so long as you stay inside the company's territory. If documents can be rocketed to your desk at work, they can be rocketed to your desk at home. In short, you wash your hands of the entire document-handling morass; when you need something, you ask for it and that's that.

Obviously no such service is possible in the physical-document world. There is no way to do it. But in the software world there *is* a way; in principle you *could* hire a company to manage your electronic documents, and be assured of getting whatever you need as soon as you ask for it, wherever you are; organizing, storing, retrieving, and delivering those documents would be the company's worry. Services vaguely like this are in fact starting to appear on the Internet—in the wrong form, so far as we are concerned, but the picture is changing fast. It's not surprising, in any case, that this sort of service never developed inside the desktop environment. It's impossible in the physical world, and paradigm drag works against it.

One more operation that isn't possible in the world of paper but might be useful if you could get it is "time travel"—restoring some particular context from the past. Imagine that you are at a conventional desk covered with conventional papers. You're looking for a report, and don't remember its title or author, but do remember that it arrived in the spring of '95. So you tell your desk "take me back to the spring of '95." The papers on your desk disappear and the entire desktop environment reverts (with a gentle *whoosh*) to the spring of '95. Intuition suggests and studies confirm that chronological-context information is valuable in managing and identifying documents—a point I will discuss later. There's no prospect of building time travel into a conventional paper environment. Time travel *is* doable and might be valuable in the software world, but paradigm drag works against it and it isn't part of today's electronic desktop.

The Internet offers possibilities that the electronic desktop ignores. It suggests directions for the future that the desktop is in no position to take advantage of. Most likely the nation's digital communication fabric will grow far more powerful over the next decade: fast, high-capacity links to the Internet will be available at home as they are today at many businesses. Phone companies, cable TV companies, or combinations of both are the likeliest organizations to bring this about. The result will be the information superhighway we read so much about. But what is it *for*? What's the point? Today's electronic desktop stands to gain little or nothing from the rise of an information superhighway.

One of the more interesting of the unexplored Internet possibilities is the "cyberstructure"—a device that is already workable in today's Internet, and will grow steadily more attractive as the Internet turns into the superhighway.

A *cyberstructure* (a term I made up, although the underlying concepts are old hat in computer science) is an assemblage of information floating in cyberspace. An "assemblage of information" means a collection of data items arranged according to some agreed scheme—a list of items that you can scan down, for example, or a table in which you can look things up. (In standard computing terminology, such an assemblage is a "data structure.") "Floating in cyberspace" is the interesting part. It means that you can see the assemblage—can look things up in it, add new items, delete old ones—no matter where you are in cyberspace. You don't know where the cyberstructure is stored, and don't care. Each data item has to be stored on some particular computer in some particular place; all the data items in a cyberstructure might be stored on one computer, or they might be spread out over many. To the user of the thing, however, its location is irrelevant. To reach out and grab a cyberstructure, you only need to know its name. You tell your computer, in effect, "show me the first data item in Ralph," and no matter where you and Ralph are, whether you are in Passaic and Ralph is in Bangkok, or vice versa, or you are both on the same block in midtown Manhattan, your computer responds with "ZEPPELIN!" Assuming, of course, that "ZEPPELIN!" is Ralph's first element. And why shouldn't it be?

Today, you keep the items that make up your personal data world on your own computer. But it might be better to store them in a cyberstructure; that way you could get at

gram to keep track of the whereabouts or identities of the other programs with which it needs to communicate.

When we first described Linda, computer scientists assumed that the complex tasks we were foisting off on the system to make things easy for the programmer would make the poor overworked system killingly inefficient. We might provide you with the world's most accommodating Executive Assistant, who bustles around smoothing your path and taking care of everything, but if it takes him ten minutes to walk down the hall, you won't necessarily be grateful. Linda programs might be easy to write, these people figured, but they are bound to run like dogs. (For a program to run like a dog is to run badly. I first heard the expression from a brilliant computer engineer at Bell Labs, who would fizz and sparkle as he described the internal structure of his latest piece of hardware, then frown wistfully when he got to the software and tell me "it runs like a dog." It's hard to get software right. Evidently in "real life" dogs are fast, but you can hardly expect computer scientists to know a thing like that. What are we, pet specialists?)

Luckily, Linda does not run like a dog. The system is built in a tricky way, and there is rarely any measurable difference in efficiency between Linda programs and programs using competing systems that make programmers work harder and cramp their styles. The field of parallel programming crossed a significant milestone in early 1995 when a large, heavily used scientific application was released not only in a conventional one-computer version but in an ensemble edition designed to run on many desktop computers simultaneously. (The program, called Gaussian 94, computes the shapes of complex molecules for chemists, biologists, and pharmacologists.) In the beginning, parallel computing was do-it-yourself—if you wanted a parallel program, you built your own. The network version of Gaussian was a milestone in the transition, which is not complete but continues to roll forward, to an age of commercially built parallel applications.

This ensemble version of Gaussian 94 was built using Linda—and of course would not have been had Linda not been simple *and* fast.

I can assert without waffling that Linda is fast because the numbers show it is, and that it is simple, which (at least to people in the field) is unarguable. We think it is elegant, too, but that is a thing I can't assert. I can discreetly point out that *other* people make this claim. But everyone reaches his own aesthetic judgments.

It is worth noting also that the Java programming language is being developed by a company called JavaSoft, and JavaSoft announced recently that it was developing a "Java-Spaces" feature modeled on Linda's tuple spaces. JavaSpaces provides operations and structures based on Linda's, and a recent JavaSoft presentation lays out a philosophy based on Linda's: that communication between separate programs, on the one hand, and long-term data storage (in files or data-bases), on the other, are two aspects of the same underlying phenomenon. When two separate programs (or people) communicate, information passes through space. When a program stores data in a file (or a person saves a notebook in a desk drawer), the intention is to pass information through *time*—to send information not from here to Peoria but from here to next Tuesday. In Linda, you can accomplish both sorts of communication, through space and through time, using the same operations. JavaSoft put it this way: "Objects over space = distribution, objects over time = persistence." The point of JavaSpaces, the company said, was to "unify and simplify."

Here is one final, less conventional attempt at getting the essence of Linda across. On the facing page is a little book-shelf I designed that resembles Linda.

One way to evaluate Linda is to consider the same under-lying design principles as applied to a different problem. The problem here is, I tend to accumulate piles of books and sketchpads wherever I go. The sofa in our living room was

always ringed with obstacles of this sort, to the extent that reaching it was like picking your way to the water on a rocky Northeastern beach at low tide. Sort of.

I needed a piece of furniture that would make books handy as I sat on the sofa. It had to be mobile, because sometimes I sit elsewhere; it had to accommodate piles of magazines, too, and have a shelf where you could put a glass, can, or handful of pencils—and the shelf's contents had to be readily disappearable, so you could make the clutter vanish without having to clean it up. It would have to accommodate a desire for well-ordered surroundings plus an equally strong desire to spend no time achieving them. (I spell this out because the Lifestreams software system to be described below has the same goal.) Some readers will be sympathetic to these requirements and some won't, but in any case they are simple and my solution is easily sized up. Color is important to the actual piece, but aside from that, the drawing gives a good account.

Each of two tipped-back shelves is divided into three bays. Each bay holds books and is just wide enough, also, to hold a face-up stack of average-size magazines. You can tip the thing back and push it like a wheelbarrow. The triangular panel on the side, below and to the rear of the top shelf, is the face of a glide-out shelf; put your hand in the half-moon cutout, pull, and the shelf comes toward you. The shelf has a vertical panel running along its rear edge and a shallow lip in front. The under-the-eaves space where the shelf retreats is a hiding place for clutter. The planks that form the book-holding surfaces and are visible from the side are warm amber; the wheels and one other pair of side panels are verdigris, the other pieces pale blue. (This verdigris is the exact color of Crayola's "sea green," which is the greatest crayon color ever invented.)

The bookshelf is like Linda because it solves the stated problem and works nicely—but if you don't like it, both facts are irrelevant. I can't prove it is a good design.

The bookcase resembles Linda also in being what appeared to me to be the cleanest, simplest solution to the given problem. Linda and the bookcase each resulted from a design-by-simplification process—and each is close, also, to the first solution I thought up. In other words, there is a strong element of whimsy in each. Each looks simple and was hard to implement. (The bookcase was built by John Lightfoot's carpentry shop.)

Linda, in any case, paves the way for cyberstructures. By making cyberstructures a practical reality on a smallish scale, Linda makes it plausible that they might work on a large scale, too. With that idea in mind, we can investigate a radical alternative to the desktop.

Our candidate for replacing the desktop is called "Lifestreams." The Lifestreams system that exists as a research prototype today was built almost entirely by Eric Freeman as a doctoral thesis project at Yale University, with significant help from Nicholas Carriero and Scott Fertig, based on an idea I first published in preliminary form in 1994. The Lifestreams system is now the basis of a vigorous commercial effort. (Its Website is "www.mirrorworlds.com.")

You may like the system or may not; it doesn't matter, because my goal is not to prove that Lifestreams is the best desktop alternative, merely to prove that there *are* alternatives. I have another goal as well—to show aesthetics in action as we stumble forward into unknown technology terrain. Whether or not you like our particular aesthetic sense, the point is that, in action, we use it as a compass; we consult it constantly. Not to be disingenuous, we of course hold Lifestreams to be a wonderful system—and it might conceivably become an important one in practice. But it would be rash to make any such prediction, and nothing in this chapter depends on the system's commercial destiny. Candidate systems like Lifestreams have played an honorable role in software history despite the long odds against any particular candidate's emerging as a real-world winner. (The Dynabook, for example, is one of the most important nonexistent objects in modern technology history. Alan Kay thought it up early in his years at Xerox PARC: a portable computer that could turn into any book you wanted by displaying pages on its high-resolution display.)

According to Lifestreams, here is your computer environment circa 2010: every document you've ever created or received stretches before you in a time-ordered stream, reaching from right now back to the date you were born. You can sit back and watch new documents arrive: they're plunked down at the head of the stream. You browse the stream by running your cursor down it—touch a document in the display and it pops out far enough for you to glance at its contents. You can go back in time, or go to the future and see what you're supposed to be doing next week or next decade. Your entire cyberlife is right in front of you.

You might be in danger of being overwhelmed by all the documents on your screen—but you use "substreaming" to describe the documents you want, and everything else (temporarily) disappears. When you want to create a new document, you spend no time deciding where to put it or what to name it. You press a button and a new element pops up at the head of the stream; you can put whatever you want inside. You can tune in your Lifestream from any Internet-connected computer, because it is stored in a cyberstructure: from your computers at work and at home (even if they are different-type machines with different operating systems), from the box that connects your TV set to the cable network, from the generic computers that will be as common as telephones today—at the supermarket, the airport, the train station, your hotel room, the ATM lobby, McDonald's, a "phone booth" on the street.

The cyberworld of 2010 is a collection of information sites. Your Lifestream is your "personal site." A newspaper or TV station, a mail-order company or tech-report cache are information sites too, and in the cyberutopia we have in mind, most such sites are stored as Lifestreams. When a Lifestream stores the electronic edition of a newspaper, today's edition goes at the streamhead with previous editions lined up behind. On a TV station Lifestream, the head element holds the latest frame of sound-and-picture. You can grab and display each new image as it emerges or watch material broadcast earlier. You carry your Lifestreams "ignition key" like an ATM or credit card; the Lifestreams card carries accounting information and a private encryption key. (The best way to protect the information stored in your Lifestream is for the system to encrypt it and hand you a physical copy of the key. The private key with which you decode your stream might be stored on the few machines you rely on most, but to reach your stream from a computer at the supermarket you will need to insert your card. The resulting system isn't airtight, but can probably be made at least as secure as the paper version of your diary.) Your Lifestreams card is a skeleton key to the cyberuniverse.

What makes this utopian picture utopian? Why is it better than today's cyberworld? Our goal in managing information is to make the time you spend managing tend to zero (maximum simplicity), as your "information power"—your capacity to find what you need and do what you want—tends to infinity (maximum power). The Lifestreams system is promising because it makes electronic *housekeeping* fast and easy (you spend minimal time organizing and arranging things) and *retrieval power* high (it's easy to find what you want and manipulate it effectively). Most important, the system promises benefits from *integration*: it allows you to accomplish many tasks using the same small repertoire of techniques. A good tool—mathematical, philosophical, gardening—has the effect of bringing to the fore deep-lying similarities among superficially different problems (planting tulips, preparing a perennial bed, digging up saplings, bopping raccoons). That is the Lifestream system's main goal.

Another Lifestreams property is more elusive but still important: the essence of a Lifestreams environment can be captured in a simple mental picture—namely, in the image of a single, all-encompassing, receding stream. When you connect to your Lifestream, the image you see on a Lifestreams-equipped Macintosh computer might be different from what you'd encounter on a PC screen—or, for that matter, on your TV or a small handheld computer (a "personal digital assistant") or the simple terminal you find at the supermarket or a pair of fancy 3D virtual-reality goggles. But your *mental* picture is what counts, not the image on the screen. Because that mental picture and the operations that go with it are simple, readily grasped, and readily held in mind, it will be easy (we believe) for users to adapt to a variety of Lifestreams dashboards, using the underlying mental picture as a guide. That adaptability in turn is a strong basis for "universal access"—the idea that your Lifestream should be accessible from any Net-connected machine anywhere regardless of hardware or operating system.

The fully realized model envisions Lifestream-provider companies working in tandem with software on your personal computer (or whatever computer you're using at the moment). The provider stores your Lifestream securely and guarantees that you can reach it when you want to.

The Lifestreams system treats your own private computer as a mere temporary holding tank for data, not as a permanent file cabinet. It takes over management of the main memory and disk on your local machine. (Of course, you can hold it off to the extent you choose, but performance will suffer accordingly.) On your own private computer, the system stores copies of the documents you are working on, the programs you are running, summary information about other documents and the stream as a whole, other documents it guesses you are likely to need soon (for example, newly arrived E-mail you haven't looked at yet), and as much of the rest of your stream as will fit. It retains up-to-date master copies of everything. If you're hard at work on your stream when a UPS truck arrives with your new computer, you can unplug your old machine and smash it to bits with a sledgehammer, hook up your new computer and continue working in your stream with no discernible blip, except for temporary delays while your suddenly empty disk and memory are refilled.

The Lifestreams model, which puts the Internet (or information highway) at the center of the computing universe, takes advantage of technological changes that are under way in any case. With or without Lifestreams, the Internet will grow in capacity, speed, and accessibility. The interesting question is: Once we've got a high-speed information highway, what will we do with it? For one, run Lifestreams.

Every chunk of information (every document, E-mail message, application transcript, Rolodex card, appointment-calendar item, and so on) is stored by this system in a single, time-ordered stream. When you tune in, you see a stream of documents receding into the distance; farther away in imaginary space means farther back in time. When you create a new document or one arrives (via E-mail, for example), you see a new document pop up at the streamhead. To create a new document, you can press the *new* button and get an empty box ready to fill, or clone an old document and get a new copy to alter as you choose. You don't need to name documents (although you can); documents are located by attribute and chronology. Attributes describe the type, point- and time-of-origin, and other aspects of a document. We count every nontrivial word in a document as an attribute, too, so we can do content-based searches. The *find* button creates a substream—you can ask for "all documents that mention zeppelins or rigid airships," "all messages from Schwartz," "the last message from Schwartz," and so on. In response, the system shows you the portion of the stream consisting only of the documents you have specified and deposits on the main stream a "calling card" document that gives you access to the new substream if you want to revisit it.

It is important that we make the documents on your stream accessible by means of more sophisticated searches also. Suppose you want to retrieve all the zeppelin-related documents on your stream (or on the publicly accessible portion of someone else's stream). You ought to be able to type the single word *zeppelin* and have the system infer that a document that never mentions "zeppelins" but *does* discuss "rigid airships" is also germane. And the system should propose documents (as a librarian might) that don't match exactly but might nonetheless be of interest: for example, those that don't discuss rigid airships but *do* mention blimps (which are, of course, nonrigid airships), or the *Hindenburg*. There was a famous zeppelin called the *Los Angeles*; most documents that mention Los Angeles will be of no interest whatsoever, and I mean *zero*, and documents that mention "*The* Los Angeles" might be using the phrase as part of a larger, irrelevant one ("The Los Angeles police department . . . "). If, on the other hand, a document mentions "The *Los Angeles*" along with other zeppelinesque turns of phrase—"lighter than air," perhaps, or "hydrogen," "helium," "control car," "Blaugas"— that is still no guarantee of relevance, but adds up to a fairly strong case.

Today's Lifestream system can't do this sort of sophisticated searching, but in a separate project we have developed exactly the software (which I describe in another book) to make it possible. Lifestreams and this "expert database" system fit together hand in glove, and the mating operation will be accomplished soon.

A substream persists until you kill it. A newly arriving zeppelin-related document gets dumped in the main stream and also appears on every substream where it fits. If Schwartz sends another message, the single member of the "last message from Schwartz" substream changes.

When you press the *squish* button, you get a summary of a substream. The type of summary depends on the type of information in the substream—textual for plain documents, graphs or pictures or animations for the appropriate more specialized types. The *squish* button automatically invokes an appropriate *squish* for this substream (or offers you a choice of reasonable squishers). (Our prototype comes with a few different *squish*es built in, but the system is intended to accommodate custom add-on squishers as well. In some cases, highly complex and sophisticated squishers will be desirable. The Lifestream system's contribution isn't to say how these squishers should be built—rather, to suggest *that* they be built, and to provide a uniform framework in which they can be installed. We anticipate a lively after-market in fancy squishers one day.) An "E-mail message" is any document copied from one stream to another. You print a document by copying it to a printer stream. (Associated with a printer, in other words, is the stream of documents it is supposed to print; unlike a typical Lifestreams user, the printer chews up its stream and destroys it as it goes along—grabs the oldest document, prints it, and repeats.) It translates its stream from "virtual" to "actual."

To run a program, you create a new document and run the program inside. Lifestreams creates a "virtual screen" that the program treats as if it were the real one; if it wants to create and manage its own windows (or wants to manage windows using a system other than Lifestreams), it can do so freely inside its virtual screen. You can have as many virtual screens on your stream as you like.

The stream has a future as well as a past. Appointments and calendar items are stored in the future, and become visible when their creation times roll around or when you go to the future on purpose to look around. You can build forward-into-the-future substreams just as you build backward-into-the-past ones. A future-looking substream selects elements from "now" forward—it might show you all your appointments for next week, or every scheduled meeting in which you are likely to see Feinstein. You can include on your stream as much of the future as you like; you might want to empty an electronic packet of institutional calendar items onto your stream (so you can ask questions like, "When does the fall term start?"); if you are a member of a museum or a fan of some team or an enthusiastic shopper at some store, you might avail yourself of the corresponding calendar packets; openings, games, and spectacular one-day sale events will now be interspersed with your own calendar items in the "future" segment of your stream, and will be accessible for examination and summary in the usual way. In the search for simplicity and power, symmetry is one of the best tools available; hence Lifestreams' symmetric treatment of past and future.

The stream, then, has three segments—past, present, and future. Ordinarily the display shows only the present and (stretching out behind it) the past; the future is visible when you ask for it. But you can also pull a lever on the display (mouse-activated, although a real lever would be nice) to reverse the stream, whereupon you see the future stretching out before you instead of the past.

Documents in the "present" can be changed or expanded. Farther back, in the "past," they have frozen into history and you can read but not change them. Each user decides when the present ends and the past begins—at what point, in other words, documents freeze. One possibility (and the system's choice unless you tell it otherwise) is to freeze today's documents at the start of tomorrow. In that case you can work on a document all day, but to continue the next day you need to clone a new copy onto the streamhead. Or a user might postpone freezing for a week, or forever. The far tail of the stream—for example, documents that are more than two years old—may disappear at the system's discretion into warehouse storage. The user specifies where the "far tail" begins, but the Lifestreams provider will presumably set charges that depend on a user's willingness to have old material dumped into warehouses. The system guarantees that the "header" of every document—the information that is available on the display when you browse but before you open a document—will always be available immediately. But if you journey to the remote past and open a document that has been archived, you may have to wait awhile until it wends its way back to daylight.

An "agent" is a program that inhabits a software system like a mouse in a kitchen; it roams around in the background, taking care of business. Your system can have many agents, and they all carry on independently. The Lifestreams system is designed to be a good home for agents, and agents handle many important Lifestreams functions. For example: an agent can cruise to the head of a stream and go to sleep after posting instructions that it be awakened whenever a new document arrives. This is the mechanism we use to assign new documents to the appropriate substreams. Custom squishers, custom agents, and custom viewports are the main ways in which the system accommodates extensions and refinements.

The stream is organized by time because it is intended to function as an electronic diary. It's not just a file cabinet for information; it tracks your daily experience as it unfolds. Such a record is inherently useful—which is why people keep journals or diaries, or used to. There is a considerable literature in industrial psychology suggesting what you know anyway, that preserving the chronological context of a document can be valuable when you are searching for it. This literature (some of which is interesting) is discussed in Eric Freeman's thesis.

You don't search for documents only on the basis of creation time, of course. And if you like conventional folders or directories, you can build them out of substreams.

In sum: under Lifestreams, the same operation that makes a directory also creates a mailbox, a hotlist of "bookmarks" that can be used for reaching Websites, a phone log, an appointment calendar. In each case, you press *squish* to create a synopsis. Browsing documents in search of a file or mailboxes in search of a letter or next week's appointments to get a feel for your schedule are three uses for the same operation. If you know how to locate the file you want (by using *find* to create a substream), you know how to set up an agent to filter your mail (incoming mail gets tossed into the appropriate substreams automatically). When you return to your machine you can tell at a glance how much mail has collected, and check through it at the sweep of a mouse. You can reorder your entire information world in a few keystrokes. Our prototype realizes all of these capacities.

That is Lifestreams, in brief. Is the system elegant? All I can say is that it is intended to be. Maybe we hit the target and maybe not, but in any case our guidelines in designing this system (and every other research system with which I have been involved) were exclusively aesthetic.

*   *   *

The Lifestreams system as a whole *is* an interface, between you and the computational universe; but the system needs to be accessible by means of a display on your screen. Many types of display are possible and no single type is ideal under all circumstances, but the "basic display" we have in mind (it exists today only in part) works like this.

It has a large center panel and smaller panels on each side. In the center you see the stream starting with the head and reaching back in time—looking like sheets of paper lined up single file, dominoes on edge. Each sheet represents one document. (Only a small fraction of the stream will fit on the display at one time.) When you touch a document with your mouse, it slips instantly out of line and expands slightly, into a "browse card"—a document summary. When you open a document, you get a window that occupies most of the center panel (hiding the perspective view underneath); each document has a "helper application" that fires up automatically when it is opened—a word processor for text documents, image viewer for pictures, and so forth. This central panel also holds the main Lifestreams controls.

The left panel has a clock and a vertical control bar representing the whole stream—the bar is labeled with the date of the stream's first document and its last (in the sense of farthest into the future). Moving a "slider" along the vertical scale causes the center-panel view to refocus on the dates under the slider. The right panel is the "card gallery": two columns of stacked-up business card–sized images, each corresponding to something you are using now or used recently. When you open a document, its browse card—a compressed overview of the document, something like an icon but larger—goes into the card gallery, on top of the card you have least recently referred to; you can reopen a document by mousing on its card. Calling cards for substreams and other people's streams go into the card gallery also, as do "live squishes" that allow you to monitor information (about the weather, say, or the stock market) continuously.

The interface is designed for any conventional computer screen. What Lifestreams would really like, though, is a three-screen flat-panel display—a large central screen with one upright-rectangular panel hinged on each side. The left side-panel would hold the vertical control bar; the right panel would hold the card gallery.

The Lifestreams system has big aspirations. It provides a simple, powerful way to maneuver around any repository of time-ordered electronic data. That capacity is potentially useful for many reasons.

Consider TV. Everyone agrees that TV is in for radical changes; the question is, will it be well or poorly integrated with the Internet-based cyberworld? Nearly everyone agrees that a TV station ought to be an archive and not just a real-time feed (in other words, that VCRs are doomed). On Tuesday at 10:00 you ought to be able to watch programs originating on Tuesday at 10:00 *or* at any previous moment. Clearly, too, you ought to be able to bring the power of your desktop computer to bear on your TV, searching through archived material, posting agents to trap what you want, stripping out commercials. But what kind of software structure should an "archival" TV station live in? How do you dial yourself backward in time? How do you search for what you want? How can schedule information be integrated with program material?

The match to Lifestreams is obvious. A Lifestream is a network-accessible archive of time-ordered information, which is exactly what a TV station will be. Imagine a Lifestream as a stack of cards; you can draw little pictures on each one, thumb the edges, and get a flip-book. Edge-thumbing is just a matter of running the right version of *squish* over the stream of TV sound-and-image frames. (The job of *squish* is, in general, to let you grasp a stream's contents without having to pull out each element and examine it individually. Animation is one way to go about it, and animation-squishers aren't restricted to video streams. Imagine a Lifestream in a medical setting, for example, where every patient has a stream that accumulates each new datum as it emerges. To get a patient's chart you merely *squish* this stream, and a clinician ought to be offered a variety of ways to do it. A squisher that converts the stream into an animated image—a moving chart or graph or illustration of some kind—might be one useful way to present a large amount of data quickly.)

Program information in the form of text documents would be interspersed with images. The "future" part of a TV stream functions as a program guide: the same operation (create a future-looking substream) that shows you your appointment calendar for next week will also work, when you apply it to a TV stream, to show you next week's programming. The same operation that dials you back to last April to scrounge around for a report can also take you back to last April to watch a movie you missed. The TV squisher can respond to commands like "fast forward" or "search for" or "rewind."

Your TV set in this worldview consists of Lifestreams running on a computer with a biggish display and the appropriate squisher. After you unpack it and plug it in, you need to find some interesting stations; you might point *find* at the outside world and type "CBS." (Suppose that you don't have the calling card for a stream you want to investigate. We already have a way of finding things—namely, *find*. Ordinarily *find* rummages through your own stream, but you can make it rummage through calling cards for everyone else's stream instead—through the calling cards of every other stream in the world that is willing to be visible to outsiders. If you want to refocus your display on Conchita Feinstein's stream but don't have her calling card, you can let *find* search the world for "Conchita Feinstein," starting with "nearby" Lifestreams and foraging farther and farther afield until it reaches Outer Mongolia, or whatever site is most distant from yours as your particular installation sees things. The result will be a substream consisting of calling cards for every Conchita Feinstein in the world—unless you see what you want and terminate *find* in mid-search, as you ordinarily would.)

If you type "CBS" to find, you would get back a stream of calling cards for "CBS" streams, and you could tune in any CBS station by clicking on its calling card in the regular way. (The same tricks work, obviously, for digital sound. You can seek out a particular recording by Alonzo and the Rap Romeos the same way you look for CBS, pay for your own copy of the stream or rent it by the hour, and set your music squisher cruising. The music stream might have program notes or video mixed in. Your card gallery might now include E-mail, the report you're working on, C-Span, E-mail from some particular person, a local radio station, and your favorite recording of the Missa Solemnis. You mouse among them in the regular way.)

Suppose you and another Lifestreams user want to chat on-line. One approach: you spawn a new Lifestream, and you each tune it in. (The streams we've discussed so far have been long-lasting, but Lifestreams can be created and destroyed on the fly as the need arises.) To make a comment, you pop a document on the stream and put your comment inside. The Lifestreams-based conversation supports any number of participants, and allows chatters to join in at any time: a third party might add new comments to a conversation that took place yesterday, assuming the original participants allowed their "conversational Lifestream" to hang around.

But notice, now, that there is no fundamental distinction between this sort of software conversation and a network bulletin board. Suppose we store bulletin boards in Lifestreams: users once again acquire the power to browse, search, and squish the same way they do at home.

Given "chatstreams," it's easy to see how phone calls could be stored on Lifestreams, too. Each party to the call runs a "phone agent" that translates speech into data packets and tosses them on a phone-call stream, while concurrently grabbing each successive packet from the stream and turning it back into sound. To phone Schwartz I would spawn a stream plus an agent, then send Schwartz the stream's calling card. If he wants to take the call he opens the stream, his own phone agent fires up, and he's in business. Phone ringing is handled by an agent that sits on the end of your stream and makes noise when a call-request document shows up. If you are in frequent phone contact with some party, you can allow the phonestream you share with him to persist; either of you can place a call (or leave a message) by reopening the shared stream.

Again, integration yields benefits. To find out what calls I've missed when I return to my machine, I build a substream of call-requests. (Callers who failed to reach me can leave answering machine–type messages on the phonestream that had been intended to hold the conversation.) Lifestreams now provides a complete filing system for phone calls and phone messages. An agent can forward my calls by copying an incoming call–request document to some other stream. If you want to identify yourself in hopes of convincing someone to take your call, you can type a message into your call-request document before shipping it off. Setting up a conference call is trivial: you send your request to many streams instead of one. Because your TV is also your phone, it can pause a program when you get a call, and pick up where you left off when the call is over.

It's widely agreed that services like phones, TV, and Internet access will be unified in the future; there's nothing new in that prediction. But merely to make the prediction begs the important questions: Will these services be *integrated*? How? How will users negotiate the new communications landscape? Will 90 percent of them make do with 2 percent of the system's power, because they can't figure out how to get the rest to work? Will the communications landscape become a slapdash, complex pastiche along the lines of today's computing landscape? "Unclarity and confusion" is what you get, recall Ted Nelson saying, when you are faced with "too many separate, unrelated things to know and understand." Do we stand a chance of achieving power and simplicity and integration?

If you master the Lifestreams dashboard, you know in essence how to deal with files and calendars, mail and phonelogs and lists of Websites—and how to work your fancy new digital TV set, how to deal with bulletin boards, how to set up a chat room or a conference call on-line (just spawn a stream and hand out calling cards). And these capacities are delivered in a context where you no longer worry about managing your file and disk space, no longer care what base operating system a machine is running and can plunge into your private information world at any gas station, karaoke bar, or Pizza Hut in the country.

Because Lifestreams undertakes such a wide variety of tasks, the number of systems it resembles in one way or another is gigantic. Relevant points of comparison include file-indexing systems, information-retrieval and -filtering systems, corporate document and archiving systems, personal information handlers, time and contact managers, workflow systems and financial managers, among others. The relationship between Lifestreams and these other applications is an important topic, which is surveyed at length in Freeman's dissertation and some of our technical papers.

SIX

Computer Ugliness

When people discuss the beauty or ugliness of computers and software, they refer almost always to the design of the interface or the internal structure of a program or machine. But computers aren't merely powerful information-transforming devices; they are objects, too—graceless, lumpy objects.

Is it frivolous to suggest that computer housings themselves should be well designed? Maybe, but I don't understand how anyone who cares a damn about the quality of his surroundings could be happy with the status quo. Almost every office in the country centers on an electronic Model T, an awkward shape that is cheap to build and enshrines permanently the first thing that came to mind. And they all look the same; their sheer sameness ought to make us suspicious. Plastic has virtues, but other materials do too. Plastic itself comes in a million flavors—opaque or clear, dull or shiny, marbled, metallic, speckled, mottled—but almost every computer on the market has the same soft dull finish and they are all the same color, more or less. When computer designers get drunk and go crazy, they dream up such wild colors as pale dove gray and intermediate eggshell, and then pass out from the sheer creative exertion.

Today's designs are boring and all the same, and they work badly, too. Your screen needs to be a foot or more away from your face, but your keyboard ought to be right under your fingers, fairly tight to the chest. Ordinarily there will be empty space between the keyboard and the bottom of your screen, because the keyboard is rather close and the screen is rather far. That's good; you badly *need* space around your computer, for the book or notepad or marked-up draft you refer to as you work, or manuals, or a telephone or a cup of coffee. So how do today's computers make use of this valuable tract of land between the keyboard and the screen? Typically they do nothing with it, they toss it in the trash. You want diskettes and CDs handy, but computers almost never supply good places to keep them. A mouse needs a pad, but the mouse pad is never built in. Some computer companies have invested heavily (to be fair) in making their boxes look nice—Apple, for example. IBM has long been a patron of good design. Silicon Graphics and a few others have made an honest effort, but none has got anywhere.

What about leading-edge computers, the next generation commercial product? Consider three examples from a recent issue of the design magazine *I.D.* The editors commend a new Toshiba computer whose dark-gray plastic monitor, keyboard, and upright-standing main box have gently swelling-out sides like square sails puffed with wind; they suggest buildings by Frank Gehry. A designer at Microsoft has a new mouse, a neat variation on the swollen-potato theme that is popular nowadays, and a new keyboard where the left-side keys are angled right and the right-side angled left, and the front edge swells out in another gentle, convex curve. Both pieces are bleached-oatmeal color. In a showy back-cover ad, a design company displays its latest laptop prototype. The screen and keyboard have gently S-curving sides. The keys are set in arching auditorium ranks, the speakers fold out on each side and (the nicest touch) a hand-rest in what seems to be pale tan suede runs along the front of the keyboard. Otherwise the machine is mostly dark gray.

All three are good designs by capable designers. All three are made of the standard plastics in the standard colors, and their parts are laid out in the standard ways. Even their modestly curvy departures from conventional are conventional.

Now let me describe some new computer-housing designs of my own. You might like them or hate them; once again, it doesn't matter. Not because I am indifferent to people's opinions; because, once again, I am attempting to establish not that any particular alternative is good but that there *are* alternatives.

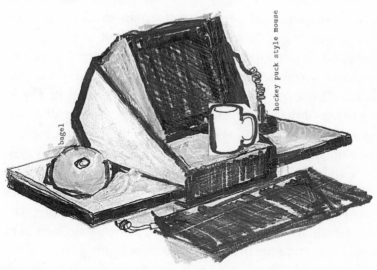

Figure 1

Figure 1 is made of warm orange wood, cherry or mahogany; you can see some of the plastic monitor housing, which is available in (let's see . . .) verdigris, mustard, or rose. The shelves below the screen and sticking out on each side serve as mouse pads or hold coffee cups. The front panel folds down for access to the diskette and CD drives. The item that looks like a hockey puck with a smokestack in the middle is the mouse; because it sprouts out the top and is connected overhead, the cord stays out of the way. You can save and refill the wooden cabinet when you upgrade the machine.

This first design is more conventional-looking than the others; the details that distinguish it from standard commercial models might be smallish, but for some people they will be important. Standard models force you to devote desk real estate to the computer, or the stuff that computer gravity attracts (the papers, mouse pads, coffee cups), but not both. The main box in this first computer takes up desk space too, but shares some of it: you can keep papers or diskettes on top of the box (there is empty space between the box-top and screen-bottom), and perch a coffee cup toward the front. The projecting shelves take up space, but you can store things on the desktop beneath them. And when people pass up plastic furniture and shell out good money for wood, they do it for a reason. The color of wood creates warmth. The irregularity of the grain makes the eye happy. Sum it all up and for some people, wood is still an irrelevant frivolity; for others ambiance is important, and subtly affects the way they work and think.

Figure 2 is designed to establish a comfortable presence on a traditional desk. The case is translucent amber plastic with tortoise shell–style veining, like a 1930s fountain pen. The desk lamp running beneath the screen lights your desktop and keyboard but doesn't wash out the display. The shelves on either side of the screen are reasonable places for a phone or books, or you might want to use them for mouse pads— but more likely you'd want the mouse closer to you, next to the keyboard.

When you aren't using the keyboard, you can stash it in the hollow along the unit's bottom. This is important if you happen to be running Lifestreams or a system with similar capacities—even if you aren't doing any active computer work, such systems show you the current state of your electronic life at all times. They show you E-mail, calendar items, and various other information chunks as they arrive. So you may want to leave your computer on all the time and glance at the screen now and then, whatever you are doing.

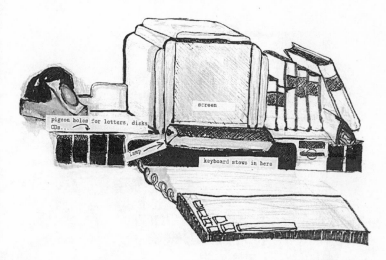

Figure 2

In Figure 3 the monitor, main box, disk drives, and speakers all hang inside a metal scaffolding—a graph-paper lattice of uniform squares. The lectern below the screen holds manuals or drafts for transcribing. There are storage nooks for books or manuals or newspapers, diskettes and CDs, pens and pencils.

Figure 3

shelves have half-circle cut-outs,
amphitheater-style

screen
(tilted back)

Figure 4

Figure 4 is a whole desk. The amphitheater-shaped shelves where the screen is embedded are designed to hold books (neatly surrounding you in three ranks) or anything else—phone, documents, whatever. (I designed this desk originally for my younger son, but in his version a globe is embedded instead of a computer screen.) The amphitheater model makes a good transition to a different sort of computer; flat-screen displays are gaining ground, and will probably supplant conventional ones before long, although conventional displays may continue to be sharper and brighter for some time. This design works equally well with a conventional or a flat screen.

Figure 5

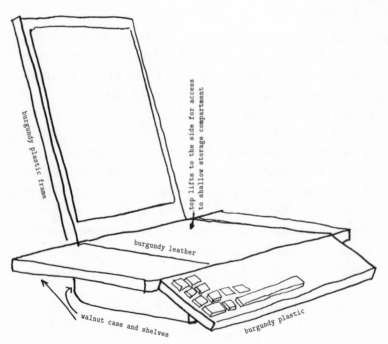

Figure 6

Figure 5 is designed for a flat screen. The "lectern" holds books, notes, or documents alongside the display; books and a phone go on top.

Figure 6 is flat-screen only—a monitor, keyboard, and wooden shelves arranged like petals on the four sides of a square wooden box. It's not a laptop, but it's easy to move around; the shelves fold over onto the box top, and the screen and keyboard unlatch. (This model has an "intermediate" portability that some people need but can rarely find. You wouldn't put it in a briefcase, but it moves easily from room to room, or you could throw it in the trunk of your car.)

I have dozens more designs on file, but I won't belabor the point. If you don't like these, pick a different designer or design your own.

If we shook up computer design, we'd arrive not only at better-looking computers and hence a better-looking world, but at better-functioning ones; upgrading aesthetics usually upgrades function, too. But the ugliness of computers is a story that goes beyond aesthetics right to the base of modern society.

Here is a classic story of modern times, an especially important one but typical nonetheless. In 1974, New York City's West Side Highway collapsed. Twenty-two years passed before ground was broken for a replacement. Why? We are ready with a stack of explanations: the case was unusual for the following million reasons. Wandering around this lush forest of special circumstances we lose sight of the amazing fact underneath—an important piece of the city broke, and two decades later we still hadn't fixed it. The only word for such a society is *passive*. We are passive in our own distinctive way: we don't loll in hammocks, we run around in circles screaming. But it makes no difference in the end.

That same passivity shapes the world of modern computers and software. I have already listed my objections to software. The computers themselves are eyesores and fit badly into the desktop landscape. Why do we put up with it?

The West Side Highway was built in 1937. The electronic marvel of the moment was radio. Radios and computers are different in many ways—radios (among other differences) were strictly for entertainment and intended to last a fair number of years. It is fascinating nonetheless that you could get your radio in wood or chrome or blue mirrors or plastic—solid plastic or marbled, opaque or translucent. Radios came in towers and globes, square or rounded, staid or swoopy; with square dials, round dials, ruler dials, half-circle dials. Fada's lovely Streamliner series alone was available in yellow, orange, orange-on-maroon, yellow-on-black, vermil-ion-on-yellow, orange-on-creamy-blue. Within a decade of the rise of commercial radio, radio-case design was an art in itself. A minor art, no question. But those exuberant radios delivered a bit of beauty and joy to their owners, and still do. The mere fact that thousands of these gorgeous things still exist is grounds for euphoria.

"Passive" is the last thing you would ever say about the society that made them.

SEVEN

Unseen Beauty

How do the pieces add up? Great technology is beautiful technology. If we care about technology excellence, we are foolish not to train our young scientists and engineers in aesthetics, elegance, and beauty. The idea of such a thing happening is so far-fetched it's funny—but, yes, good technology is terribly important to our modern economy and living standards and comfort levels, the "software crisis" is real, we do get from our fancy computers a tiny fraction of the value they are capable of delivering: we are a nation of Ferrari drivers tooling around with kinked fuel lines at fifteen miles per hour. We ought to start teaching Velázquez, Degas, and Matisse to young technologists right now on an emergency basis. Every technologist ought to study drawing, design, and art history. Ugly software—hence weak, late, broken, or obnoxious software—would still get built even if we did. Art education is no magic wand. But I can guarantee that such a course of action would make things better: our technology would improve, our technologists would improve, and we would never regret it.

(Of course, art history in the colleges nowadays often seems like mud wrestling, as posturing professors who care not at all about truth and beauty and a lot about politics, ideology, and social agendas drag art down to their level, and the whole field sinks slowly into the slime: you can only shake your head and wonder. It's easy to forget that every serious art history department in the country still harbors a few professors who love art; those people could do as much as anyone to pull us out of our software crisis.)

By and large, we go about computer science education in the wrong way; not surprising, given that the academic field was dreamed up during the 1960s and early '70s under radically different circumstances from the ones that hold today. We ought to teach basic programming in studios: students ought to build the same simple programs repeatedly until each one is not merely correct and efficient but elegant. Passing students on the basis of mere technical adequacy yields badly trained programmers and a software crisis; we'd have a piano crisis, too, if music students moved from one finger exercise to the next the instant they succeeded in hitting the right notes. Advanced students ought to present their software projects as architects-in-training do, to juries capable of aesthetic judgments. The projects we assign ought to be based (again, as in architecture school) on real projects in the real world.

Some people are born with and some without an acute sense of beauty, but anyone's beauty sense can be improved by training. The best training is the study of art—art being the freest pursuit of truth and beauty for their own sakes that humans are capable of. Art education is crucial to the nation's technological and scientific well-being. Not because ignorance of Velázquez (say) makes a person incapable of doing physics; because studying Velázquez sharpens the sense of beauty, which in turn helps guide physicists toward the truth. Art study to a scientist or engineer is like jogging to a boxer. It is no replacement for mathematics or assiduous punching-bag smashing, but it develops a faculty that is crucial to success.

The closeness of art and science sheds light on today's art education also. Nowadays the prestigious art schools spurn technique and see it as their mission to put students in touch with their feelings—equivalent to training chemists not by teaching them chemistry but by sending them straight into the lab to have fun. Fooling around happens to be essential in learning science or art. But to teach it *instead of* technique is just as disgraceful and stupid in art school as it would be in science education and is yet another sign of our refusal to take art seriously, another breach of faith with our students, whom we betray in a million ways daily.

It is a tragedy that science and technology's overwhelming success has convinced many people—some of whom will even admit it—that art is an anachronism, that science and technology are the only intellectual attainments that count. We are up in arms about the pathetic state of math and science education in our schools, and are right to be; that the average American schoolchild emerges from high school and (in due course) college knowing nothing about art doesn't bother us. But technology's growing centrality throughout economic and intellectual life makes it *more* and not less important that students study art.

Of course, you cannot learn computer science for real, cannot aspire to do research, unless you have mastered a fair amount of math and computation theory. Professional programmers need some math, too, so they can analyze the performance of their programs, and as a general guide to straight thinking. My computer-science-education-of-the-future offers mathematics and computation theory, of course, just as the Bauhaus offered metalworking and wood shop. Computer science training is in fact merely one element of my brand-new three-part university of the future. The "Aesthetics School" teaches computation and mathematics, physics and engineering, design, art, architecture, and music. The "Literature School" centers on good writing and deep reading and teaches history, philosophy, religion, psychology, law, and foreign languages, treating each as a branch of literature. The Biology and Medicine School takes up the slack. And by all means help yourself to an Economics and Business school, too, if you'd like.

Radical suggestions, and I'm not holding my breath. But the bright side of the software crisis, and the far more important crisis of our universities in general, is that things *must* change. Today's colleges will change dramatically in our lifetimes whether they choose to or not. In their current state they are unsustainable. The change I hope will *not* happen is the simple cracking-apart and breaking-up of the humanities and social sciences, like ice floes in spring, at all except a few top schools; but I wish my academic colleagues would grasp that such an outcome is possible. If the prostitution of scholarship to politics in research *and* teaching goes much farther, students and their parents and the taxpayers are going to stop paying for it.

Great technology is beautiful technology. The main reason to understand that fact is not the software crisis but the opportunity to feel more deeply the beauty that lies around you. What could be sadder than to live in a beautiful world and never know it?

Machine beauty is an important part of modern intellectual life; the beauty paradox is, too. It isn't just that the Xerox bigwigs rejected the Alto desktop and then most computer users rejected the Macintosh desktop, and then Microsoft brought out a new product and computer customers changed course and flipped around like a school of minnows; not just the software experts who insist that mathematics and not aesthetics points the way forward, despite the evidence; not just the relentless drive in the industry to complicate and featurize every piece of software until it keels over out of sheer brainless ugliness. It is our wider failure to see the importance of aesthetics to our whole scientific and technological enterprise.

If beauty is so important and so many scientists and technologists *say* it is, what makes us treat aesthetics as irrelevant and frivolous? In part, it is merely the times; we act dumb because we are dumb. As our schools and colleges teach less and less, our national knowledge level recedes. U.S. civilization dries out, bakes and cracks like parched soil—tears itself into separate islands, the science island and the art island separated by a channel of dust, each one barren and dead. An educated person used to learn something about art and music and literature and science and mathematics as a matter of course. Technical people knew at least a little about art, nontechnical ones at least a bit about science and mathematics.

The devastation wrought by a full generation of educational appeasement is awful and largely invisible. You rarely notice a patch of soil drying out; it hits you only after the fact that plants used to grow on that square of dust, ages ago. Why is today's TV comedy less funny than Sid Caesar's in the 1950s? As far as Larry Gelbart is concerned (he worked for Caesar), it's simple: "audiences used to be smarter, more educated, and now they have been dumbed down, along with the comedies written for them." Out of sheer arrogant carelessness, we have made life worse in a million ways, small, medium, and large. We can still revive this cultural desert if we choose, but not with a watering can; big measures are called for. My personal recommendation for today's educational system—many others feel the same way—is that we tear it down with a bulldozer and begin again.

Of course, the beauty paradox involves other forces, too, many of them far older than the crisis of American education. The idea that beautiful technology is effeminate goes back a long time. The idea that technology is just inherently bad goes back to the start of the industrial revolution—and a person who hates technology is unlikely to be charmed by its beauty. Cattle ranchers are no great fans of wolfly beauty, either.

It goes without saying that there are technologies we would be better off without. But the badness rarely lies in the technology; it is almost always a matter of bad chemistry between the technology and the ambient culture. America would almost certainly be a happier, better place if (on some enchanted evening at the stroke of midnight) TV were to vanish without a trace. Run through the thought experiment for yourself: reading surges, families converse and get out of the house more, the cultural trash level recedes dramatically. Similar things happened after such big ecological successes as the cleanup of the Hudson River, which at one point was as choked with poison as today's U.S. culture. It is hard not to get wistful over an idea so wonderfully promising. And yet no serious person would ever propose a law to ban TV. It's not merely that free societies shouldn't work that way, and in practical terms (consider Prohibition) cannot. More important is a flaw in the premise: if a consensus could somehow be assembled in favor of banning TV, if many Americans were indeed offended by TV, no legal action would be necessary because TV wouldn't *be* offensive. Technology only highlights and underlines the text it is given.

When you contemplate the evils of technology, my advice is to think liquor. Liquor is old technology, granted; but those of us without special training are no more likely to be capable of producing a fifth of whiskey (or the bottle to put it in), given the raw materials, than we are a Stealth Bomber. Liquor technology is old but not trivial.

Liquor brings out the worst in us. TV does too, and so do computers. Used wisely, on the other hand, liquor produces a modicum of pleasure and makes life somewhat better, and the same holds for computers and TV. In any case, it is absurd to describe liquor itself (or any other technology) as inherently good or evil; those attributes pertain to human beings only. And to hate technology is in the end to hate humanity, to hate yourself, because technology is what human beings do. They make liquor. They build computers. Technology is the bird's nest, beaver's dam, ant's hill—creatures do what they can to make their lives more comfortable.

Most Americans, I think, neither love technology nor hate it; they like it when it serves a good purpose, dislike it otherwise. No other intelligent position exists. Yet, admittedly, technology hatred does tinge today's cultural climate with a faint noxious odor, the smell of burning rubber in the distance—this being the sort of age in which a high-ranking government official like Mr. Bruce Babbitt "would love," he says, "to be the first Secretary of the Interior to tear down a really large dam"—and technology hatred accounts for some part of the beauty paradox, too.

Of course, a glass of soda water in the sunlight, with pinprick bubbles streaming to the surface in bright columns to disappear, is beautiful, too. And if people rarely notice it, that is not because we are poorly educated about or prejudiced against seltzer.

But I don't intend to conclude mournfully.

The deep beauty masterpieces of earlier generations were no more beautiful, necessarily, than our own. But we can see them whole and understand their historical positions clearly. I have mentioned the remarkable radios of the 1930s. Sitting in my living room is an Emerson model built in 1938. It works fine but we rarely listen to it; 1938 radios are not easy to maintain. Merely sitting in silence, however, it radiates such intense vibrant energy it could knock a person over. It is an extraordinary aesthetic achievement: the layers of science, technology, and art that interact like the lines of an irresistible allegro fugue to bring this object about, the brilliant culture that created this thing and used it all speak compellingly from the small upright plastic box. Let's go for a quick walking tour—the best way to conclude a discussion of beauty in today's technology is with a pilgrimage to the sort of object that inspires and moves us; that shows us how the game ought to be played.

The radio is roughly a foot tall, of opalescent yellow plastic; the material is translucent to a depth of perhaps an eighth of an inch, and you see flashes of silvery yellow against a warmer, orangey ground. Plastics emerged in a big way in the late 1920s; in 1927 the Bakelite patent expired and other manufacturers were free to enter the market. Prices came down and bright colors emerged. (Bakelite had ordinarily been supplied in black or dark brown, but is by nature a "clear, glassy, resin-like material," as chemist and science-popularizer Gerald Wendt explained in 1939. The dark coloring in Bakelite was intended to disguise fillers that were included for strength; by the late 1920s you could make plastics that didn't need fillers.) In 1927, the American Catalin Corporation celebrated the expiration of the Bakelite patent by announcing a new plastic—an "insoluble, infusible cast phenolic resin of gem-like beauty and an unlimited color range," according to a magazine ad. Catalin was perfect for radios.

(Bakelite and related plastics like Catalin are, for Wendt, perfect examples of beautiful technology—they have "a thousand uses" and are made of coal. "The tar that forms when coal is distilled contains many different products, one of the most important being benzol, which is very easily converted to phenol, or carbolic acid. This is one of the two constituents of this Bakelite resin. The other constituent is formaldehyde, which can be very simply made by the partial oxidation of 'water gas,' made from coke and water.")

The dial is copper, lights up when the radio is turned on, and is covered with a clear plastic bubble. In the late 1930s families gathered around the radio as they might have around a hearth, and this particular model has the warmth of a pint-sized, *moderne* hearth with its yellow case, silvery ochre grillcloth and lit-up copper dial. A radio, of course, could be a pseudo-hearth in a way TV cannot. You needn't watch a radio; you can dip into its zone of radiance even if your attention is largely elsewhere.

The first table-radio generation in the early 1930s tended to have upright wooden cases shaped (when seen head-on) like pointed Gothic arches. The Emerson 1938 model stands on the boundary between Gothic wood and the freewheeling plastic boxes, usually horizontal and often rounded, that came next. The Emerson stands upright and the speaker housing is divided by the plastic grill into three vertical panels—Gothicy features. There are three smooth knobs along the bottom, for volume, tuning, and band selection, AM or "police band."

Radio physics is a huge topic, taking in as it does much of electromagnetism. There is enough to it for several years' worth of college study. But the gist is simple, and too beautiful to leave to physics majors. Here are a few scattered glimpses—as if you were catching sight of a spectacular waterfall from a speeding train miles away. The resulting view is not much, but with luck it leaves you with the impression (or reminds you) that here is a spot worth visiting at leisure. The loveliness of the place centers on the simplicity and power of the mental structure built by physics over the centuries, and the deep interconnections physics has established among an amazing range of natural and man-made phenomena.

The art represented by the Emerson radio centers on waves: as when you drop a pebble in water, or roil the atmosphere by strumming your vocal cords. *Waves* like the sine wave you drew in trigonometry class; the Emerson radio is connected via sine waves to everything else in the world or in your mind that has to do with spinning at a constant rate: to a generator, a lasso, a merry-go-round. *Waves* as in "light waves": when you tune a radio you are taking tiny, sidling steps up and down a spectrum that extends all the way down to the alternating current that comes out of your wall outlet and upward through visible light and beyond, to the ultrashort realm of cosmic rays from outer space; in principle, you could build an elegant yellow plastic receiver for light rays, X rays, or cosmic rays if you wanted to, but there is nothing much to listen to at those frequencies.

Why not? How do traffic-helicopter updates and mouthwash commercials get into radio waves in the first place, and what are they doing there? Sound comes in waves, of course—pressure waves, sliding forward through the air. The idea of a sound wave is remarkable in itself: a disturbance traveling through a basically standing-still population. The disturbance travels (it is a thing in its own right) even though the individuals do not. Sliding energy: as a child glides down a hill on a sled, energy slides through space on a wave. People can be a medium for pressure waves: merely line a bunch up, spaced maybe eight inches apart, and give the first one a shove. A pressure wave travels down the line, just as a wave of stopped traffic travels down a crowded highway or a compression wave glides through a Slinky or a jiggle slides through Jell-O. The goal of radio is to transport pressure waves from people's mouths (or some other sound source) in the studio to your ears. Wave delivery is the point.

Pressure waves themselves dissipate quickly in the atmosphere, so we can't broadcast *them*. How to deliver these waves? We could mail them, could simply transcribe the sound waves and send you a copy. Edison developed a simple way to do it: you can copy down sound waves by attaching a needle to a diaphragm and passing a soft surface (say tinfoil) under the needle. When you let the sound waves jostle your diaphragm, you get a direct transcription, a tinfoil image of the waves—otherwise known as a primitive phonograph record. (You could transcribe other mechanical waves in basically the same way. Suppose you wanted to make a record of the ripples in your child's wading pool; you could send a ripplegram to the doting grandparents. They would play it on the Ripplegraph set up in their own empty wading pool and the original ripples would be reconstructed, just as if the grandchildren were frolicking in there. Pool ripples aren't pressure waves and you would have to record them using a floating, bobbing stylus of some kind, but the principle is the same.)

The mails are not your only alternative, of course. Broadcasting sound waves is a bad strategy because they are inefficient energy movers, but electromagnetic waves are the Federal Express of energy delivery. After all, we can see stars, which is amazing when you think about it. Your retina is a radio receiver pretuned to the high-frequency band we call visible light, and is capable of picking up stations that are many light-years away. Those are powerful stations, of course; not many local stations are fusion-powered. But it gives you an inkling nonetheless. Electromagnetic waves are an impressive energy-shipping mechanism.

Could we translate sound waves into electromagnetic waves? Easily; that is what a microphone does. We could use a microphone to translate or "transduce" pressure waves into electrical waves. At the other end, we would use essentially the same device hooked up backward—namely, a speaker—to translate electrical waves back into sound.

You could take the electrical waves that come out of a microphone, send them flying off into space, and call that radio. But sound waves are relatively low-frequency, long-wavelength creatures. To make audible sounds, you vibrate in the range of 20 to 20,000 times per second. Electrical waves modeled directly on sound waves would be hard to transmit with enough power; it's easier to get the signal out at a higher frequency. Even if this weren't so, you still wouldn't want to broadcast audio-frequency waves. You would still want to convert them into some other frequency, because you can transmit only one signal per frequency (assuming that your receiving antennas gather signals from many directions at once), and you'd like to have lots of radio stations. Given the capacity to choose a transmitting frequency other than the original, ten different radio stations can choose ten different frequencies.

So you have a low-frequency wave and want to translate it into a high-frequency one—want to capture the big wave's shape using small waves as your raw material, so you can broadcast small waves but allow the receiver to reconstruct the original large ones. You use the shape of the (electrical version of) the sound wave to *modulate* the high-frequency radio waves—to mold sound-wave shapes out of radio waves. The AM band uses "amplitude modulation"; FM stands for "frequency modulation." If you were broadcasting light instead of radio waves, amplitude modulation would look like changes in brightness, frequency modulation like changes of color. An AM station broadcasting light would vary the brightness of its signal as the shape of the sound wave varied. (The navy used to flash Morse code messages between ships using signal lanterns, a short light burst for a dot and a longer one for a dash. Those lanterns were AM radio stations—they used a simple kind of amplitude modulation to send information via electromagnetic wave. A traffic light is an FM radio station. It uses changes of color—of frequency, that is—to send information.)

Electrical or "electromagnetic" waves are the heart of radio and, of course, many other phenomena. But radio (and TV and radar, among other things) exist because some brilliant physicists (notably Michael Faraday, James Clerk Maxwell, and Heinrich Hertz) mapped out the phenomenon for the sheer hell of it—for the intellectual and aesthetic satisfaction.

Most people are accustomed to thinking of electricity in terms of direct current. Create a simple electric circuit using a battery—run a wire from one pole of the battery to one end of a resistance (anything that sucks up electric energy—a lightbulb, say), and from the other end of the resistance back to the other pole of the battery. You've built a D.C., or direct current, circuit—the circuit is a one-way street for electricity, with the current running in the same direction all the way around.

But suppose you replace the battery with a source of alternating current, the sort you get from a wall outlet. With an A.C. source, the voltage (or electric pressure) oscillates instead of holding still, and as a result the current oscillates, too. A typical A.C. power source oscillates at a frequency of 60 cycles per second.

Power companies generate A.C. instead of D.C. because A.C. is easier to deliver over power cables, and the voltage of an A.C. power source is easily adjusted using transformers. When we switched from A.C. to D.C., however, we didn't just get an oscillating source of power; we got *waves*.

Compare two horses on a merry-go-round, a stander and a jumper. The stander is the D.C. horse: if you plant yourself in front of a merry-go-round and fix your gaze on a stander as it revolves from left to right in your field of view, the stander traces a straight line. Now focus your attention on a jumper; it traces an undulating wave. An A.C. power source is an up-and-down voltage jumper. It sends a wave of voltage flowing down a wire—or, more accurately, creates waves in an electromagnetic field that cause voltage and current effects in the wire.

And, remarkably enough, the shape of the radio or power wave that rolls through space or down a wire is basically the same as the shape of the wave traced by a merry-go-round jumper. Both are sine waves. A typical A.C. generator works by forcing a coil of wire to spin inside a magnetic field. The spinning causes a voltage to be set up in the coil, and the voltage varies as the coil rotates. The voltage variation produced by this sort of uniformly rotating system is shaped like a sine wave: in fact, *is* a sine wave—a sine wave being merely the shape you get when you twirl a line at a uniform rotational speed (for instance, by spinning a rock on a rope over your head) and chart the variation in apparent length of the rope when you look at it head-on.

The typical merry-go-round jumper is driven by exactly the same sort of system; it is the result of uniform circular motion. Use energy to create and maintain uniform circular motion and you have several choices—you can have an A.C. generator or a merry-go-round, depending on the context in which your rotor spins. The top of the horse pole is connected to a sort of pedal; as the pedal cranks around, the pole is driven up and down. (By the same token but in reverse, a bicycle rider drives his legs up and down and they make the pedals spin.) The main merry-go-round motor makes the platform revolve, which in turn makes the "pedals" spin and the horses pump.

The top of the jumper pole traces out a sine wave. Sine waves have to do with triangles, surveying, and so forth as well, and it is obvious why they should. Imagine someone twirling a line overhead. You chart the variation in its apparent length and get a sine wave. As the rope twirls, you know at each point (or you *could* know if you wanted to) the exact angle at which it is jutting out from the twirler's body. At o degrees it is pointing straight toward you and the apparent length is o; at 5 degrees it is longer, 10 degrees longer still, and so on. These observations are the raw material for a table of sines, and you are now ready to set up shop as a surveyor. If you want to know the distance between you and a point across the field, and you have an assistant hold a ten-foot pole straight up right at that point, and you determine that an imaginary line from your eye to the top of the pole would make a 5-degree angle with the ground . . . the rest is simple.

There is much more to be said about sine waves (they would make a nice book in themselves)—but back to the radio. A.C. power comes in sine waves, and so do radio signals. Power waves are low frequency, long and unmodulated. Radio waves are higher frequency, shorter, and molded into the shape of sound. Power waves stay bottled up inside wires and various electrical devices—but radio waves need to go barreling off into space. You can send waves into space by, for example, connecting a generator to a pair of parallel wires; the signal sloshes down the wires and out the far ends—in roughly the sense that, if you connect a sound-wave generator to the end of a cardboard tube, the sound waves go barreling down the tube and fly off into space. You can turn a tube into a megaphone by flaring the ends—that way, you give the sound source the opportunity to work harder, move more air, and make a louder noise. You can do a similar trick with a transmitting antenna. (A megaphone *is* a transmitting antenna, for sound waves.) At the receiving end, you sense electromagnetic waves using another antenna. (Put a megaphone to your ear and you get a receiving antenna for sound waves—a simple hearing aid.) Focus on the right frequency, turn the radio-frequency signal back into audio frequency, use the jiggling diaphragm of a speaker to turn the audio-shaped electrical wave into atmospheric pressure waves and you're done.

It's not all sweetness and light. The details are complicated and go far beyond the topics I have touched on here. The details of science and engineering (as of music, often, or painting or poetry) *are* difficult and complex. And if you hum the sweetest, simplest melody you can think of, the waveform that captures the physical reality will be immensely complicated. You need to master the details if you want to understand engineering or science. But you needn't allow the power and simplicity of the underlying melody to get lost.

As for the Emerson radio, it deserves to be in a museum, but how would you display it? Stick it on a pedestal under a spotlight and the case would catch the eye, but such a tactic gets you only so far. The pizzazz of the case and the strength and assurance and cultural self-respect that undergirded it are important, but so are the physics and engineering of radio, the chemistry and engineering of metals and plastics, the sounds this box would have delivered when it was new: bulletins of the world's falling apart, but Glenn Miller and Benny Goodman also, hit songs by Gershwin, Kern, and

Berlin, gossip and silly ads, the NBC Symphony under Toscanini, the Fred Astaire hour, the Chiquita commercial and its singing bananas: the whole package is part of this radio. The radio is gorgeous. You've got to hand it to us in the end, we human beings; at our best, we've got a lot of class.

=NOTES

Chapter 1: Deep Beauty

Page 2, ACCORDING TO REPORTER-AUTHOR JOHN MCPHEE: John A. McPhee, *The Survival of the Bark Canoe* (New York: Farrar, Straus and Giroux, 1975), p. 61.

Page 3, OSCAR WILDE WROTE: Cited in Richard G. Wilson, Dianne H. Pilgrim, and Dickran Tashjian, *The Machine Age in America, 1918–1941* (New York: Brooklyn Museum in association with Abrams, 1986), p. 247.

Page 3, AVERAGE BULLFIGHTERS, HEMINGWAY WROTE: Ernest Hemingway, *Death in the Afternoon* (New York, Scribner's, 1932), p. 14.

Page 3, "IF THE DANCE IS RIGHT," FRED ASTAIRE SAID: Bob Thomas, *Astaire, the Man, the Dancer* (New York: St. Martin's Press, 1984), p. 27.

Page 3, "VIGOROUS WRITING IS CONCISE," WILLIAM STRUNK WROTE: Cited in E. B. White, *Essays of E. B. White* (New York: Harper & Row, 1979), p. 258.

Page 4, WRITES THE ART HISTORIAN C. EDISON ARMI: C.

Edison Armi, *The Art of American Car Design* (University Park, Penn.: Penn State Press, 1988), p. 85.

Page 4, DAVID BILLINGTON DESCRIBES THE SWISS ENGINEER ROBERT MAILLART'S: David P. Billington, *Maillart's Bridges: The Art of Engineering* (Princeton, N.J.: Princeton University Press, 1979), p. 3.

Page 5, "BEGINNING WITH TELFORD'S 1812 ESSAY ON BRIDGES": David P. Billington, *The Tower and the Bridge: The New Art of Structural Engineering* (New York: Basic Books, 1983), p.6.

Page 5, WERE TO UNCOVER THE DAM, FEYNMAN WRITES: Richard Phillips Feynman, Robert B. Leighton, and Matthew Sands, *The Feynman Lectures on Physics* (Reading, Mass.: Addison-Wesley, 1965), Chap. 16, p. 19.

Page 6, AN ENGLISH VISITOR WROTE IN 1936 OF HOOVER DAM: Richard G. Wilson, Dianne H. Pilgrim, and Dickran Tashjian, *The Machine Age in America, 1918–1941* (New York: Brooklyn Museum in association with Abrams, 1986), p. 11.

Page 8, "A USEFUL OBJECT HAS A 'NATURAL' FORM," ONE DESIGNER WRITES: Niels Diffrient, "Design and Technology," in D*esign Since 1945*, ed. Kathryn B. Hiesinger and George H. Marcus (Philadelphia: Philadephia Museum of Art, 1983), p. 12.

Page 8, WROTE PHILIP JOHNSON IN HIS INTRODUCTION: Philip Johnson, *Machine Art* (New York: Museum of Modern Art, 1934; Arno Press reprint edition, 1969), unpaginated.

Page 11, "WEIGHT IS THE ENEMY . . . WHATEVER SAVES WEIGHT": C. Edison Armi, *The Art of American Car Design* (University Park, Penn.: Penn State Press, 1988), p. 79.

Page 13, THE ROOF LEAKED, AND THE ONLY POSSIBLE VERDICT: see Alan Holgate, *The Art in Structural Design, an Introduction and Sourcebook* (New York: Oxford University Press, 1986), p. 131.

Page 13, "THE ENGINE WAS A SHOWPIECE": Ralph Stein,

The Great Cars (New York: Grosset and Dunlap, 1967), p. 48.

Page 13, "PASSING HIS PALM FONDLY ALONG THE HOOD": James Lord, *Picasso and Dora: A Personal Memoir* (New York: Farrar Straus Giroux, 1993), p. 47.

Pages 13–14, "AS CARS WERE DRIVEN MORE RAPIDLY BY MORE EFFICIENT MOTORS": Cited in James J. Flink, *The Automobile Age* (Cambridge, Mass.: MIT Press, 1988), p. 235.

Page 14, "AN AUTOMOBILE STYLIST IS AN ADVOCATE OF CHANGE": Cited in David Gartman, "Harley Earl and the Art and Color Section: The Birth of Styling at General Motors," in *Design History: An Anthology*, ed. Dennis P. Doordan (Cambridge, Mass.: MIT Press, 1995), p. 135.

Page 17, ROGER PENROSE . . . WRITES OF THE KEY IDEA: Roger Penrose, *The Emperor's New Mind: Concerning Computers, Minds, and the Laws of Physics* (Oxford: Oxford University Press, 1989), p. 105.

Page 17, WRITES THE PHYSICIST J. R. PIERCE: Cited in David Halliday and Robert Resnick, *Physics* (New York: Wiley, 1966), p. 963.

Page 17, "WE COULD BRING FORTH THIS FORMULA": Richard Phillips Feynman, Robert B. Leighton, and Matthew Sands, *The Feynman Lectures on Physics* (Reading, Mass.: Addison-Wesley, 1965), Chap. 22, p. 1.

Page 17, "THE MOST PRECISE AND BEAUTIFUL DEFINITION": Ibid., Chap. 12, p. 1.

Page 18, THE ART HISTORIAN WILLIAM RUBIN SPEAKS: William Rubin, ed., *Picasso and Portraiture: Representation and Transformation* (New York: Museum of Modern Art, 1996), p. 90.

Page 18, THE JOURNAL *SOCIAL TEXT* . . . DEVOTED A RECENT ISSUE: Spring/Summer 1996.

Page 18, "PHYSICAL 'REALITY,' NO LESS THAN SOCIAL 'REALITY,'": Cited in "Professor Sokal's Trangression," *The New Criterion*, June 1996 (vol. 14, no. 10): 1.

Page 19, "THE UNJUSTIFIED CONFERRAL OF EXPERTISE":

Andrew Ross, "Introduction," *Social Text*, Spring/Summer 1996, p. 4.

Page 20, HERE IS GARRY WILLS: Garry Wills, "Homer's Women," *The New Yorker*, January 27, 1997, p. 74.

Page 22, A 1996 ESSAY COLLECTION EDITED BY TERRY WINOGRAD: *Bringing Design to Software* (New York: ACM [Association for Computing Machinery] Press, 1996).

Page 22, THE INFLUENTIAL 1990 ESSAY COLLECTION: Theodor Holm Nelson, "The Right Way to Think About Software Design," in *The Art of Human-Computer Interface Design*, ed. Brenda Laurel (Reading, Mass.: Addison-Wesley, 1990), pp. 236, 243.

Page 22, IN OUR 1990 PROGRAMMING LANGUAGE TEXT-BOOK: David Gelernter and Suresh Jagannathan, *Programming Linguistics* (Cambridge, Mass.: MIT Press, 1990), pp. 216–21.

Page 22, ALAN PERLIS WROTE: Alan Perlis, "The American Side of the Development of Algol," in ACM SIGPLAN History of Programming Languages Conference, SIGPLAN Notices, August 1978 (vol. 13, no. 8): 12.

Page 25, A NEW AIRPORT IS SCHEDULED TO OPEN IN DENVER: this and the other examples cited in this paragraph are from W. Wayt Gibbs, "Software's Chronic Crisis," *Scientific American*, September 1994, pp. 86ff.

Page 27, "INTUITION IS SLOWLY YIELDING TO ANALYSIS": Ibid., p. 87.

Page 27, "ANYONE WHO WANTS TO ANALYZE THE PROPERTIES OF MATTER IN A REAL PROBLEM": Richard Phillips Feynman, Robert B. Leighton, and Matthew Sands, *The Feynman Lectures on Physics* (Reading, Mass.: Addison-Wesley, 1965), Chap. 39, p. 2.

Page 27, "THE GERMAN EMPHASIS ON CALCULATIONS": David P. Billington, *The Tower and the Bridge: The New Art of Structural Engineering* (New York: Basic Books, 1983), p. 151.

Page 28, COMPUTERS ARE TOOLS FOR "AUGMENTING HU-

MAN INTELLECT": Howard Rheingold, *Tools for Thought: The People and Ideas Behind the Next Computer Revolution* (New York: Computer Book Division/Simon & Schuster, 1985), p. 197.

Page 29, "ALMOST NO ONE SEEMS TO BE ABLE TO RECOGNIZE *GOOD* DESIGN": Theodor Holm Nelson, "The right way to think about software design," in *The Art of Human-Computer Interface Design*, ed. Brenda Laurel (Reading, Mass.: Addison-Wesley, 1990), p. 236.

Chapter 2: The Paradox of Beauty

Page 31, THE COMPUTER WITH THE "EXTREMELY ELEGANT OPERATING SYSTEM": Mark S. Jennings, "Evaluating the Macintosh Finder," *Byte* (December 1984): A101.

Page 31, "THE REALLY FINE SOFTWARE HAS ALWAYS BEEN ON THE MAC": Cited in *IEEE* [Institute of Electrical and Electronics Engineering] *Computer* 29, no. 5 (May 1996): 10.

Page 32, "APPLE'S MACINTOSH OFFERS A SUPERIOR USER INTERFACE": "The Apple Macintosh Computer," *Byte* (February 1984): 53.

Page 33, "MANY USERS HAVE PROBLEMS REMEMBERING THE SYNTAX OF EVEN": Stan Miaskowski, "Looking Beyond the DOS Prompt," *Byte IBM Special Edition* (Fall 1989): 105.

Page 34, THE DESIGN PRINCIPLE I CALLED *ESPALIER:* David Gelernter, *Mirror Worlds* (New York: Oxford University Press, 1991).

Page 35, THEY SIGNED THE MOLD FOR THE COMPUTER'S PLASTIC HOUSING: See Steven Levy, *Insanely Great: The Life and Times of the Macintosh, the Computer That Changed Everything* (New York: Viking Penguin, 1994), p. 153.

Page 35, "REAL ARTISTS SHIP": Ibid., p. 165.

Page 36, "THE BEST DON'T ALWAYS WIN": Peter Passel, "Why the Best Doesn't Always Win," *New York Times Magazine*, May 5, 1996, p. 60.

Page 36, "COMPUTER BOXES ARE—COMPUTER BOXES": Randall Stross, "Poisoned Apple," *The New Republic*, April 22, 1996, p. 19.

Page 36, WINDOWS 3.0 IS A "MACINTOSH-STYLE SYSTEM . . .": *Consumer Reports*, September 1993, p. 570.

Page 36, "MICROSOFT," THE *NEW YORK TIMES* REPORTED, IS "THE COMPANY . . .": John Markoff, "Beyond the PC: Apple's Promised Land," *New York Times*, November 15, 1992, sec. 3, p. 1.

Page 37, BY 1993, SALES OF WINDOWS SOFTWARE: Steven Levy, *Insanely Great: The Life and Times of the Macintosh, the Computer That Changed Everything* (New York: Viking Penguin, 1994), p. 279.

Page 38, USERS OF DOS PCs REJOICE!: Jon Udell, "Three's the One," *Byte* (June 1990): 122, 126.

Page 39, "BETTER THAN THE MICROSOFT CORPORATION'S WINDOWS 3.0": Peter H. Lewis, "Personal Computers; Putting the Cart Before the Horse," *New York Times*, November 26, 1991, sec. C, p. 7.

Page 40, "THEY WILL FIRST BE STRUCK BY ITS . . . CUTENESS": Robert Nichols, "Who Wants Cute?" *InfoWorld*, March 26, 1984, p. 8.

Page 40, "IN THE BEGINNING, THERE WAS THAT CUTE MAC": Chris Albertson, "Tutorials for the Rest of Us; Macintosh Training," *MacWeek*, September 13, 1988 (vol. 2, no. 37), p. 42.

Page 40, "WHEN THE CUTE LITTLE MACINTOSH FIRST KNOCKED": Conrad Blickenstorfer, "Why the Mac Will Win," *Computerworld*, January 25, 1988, p. 61.

Page 40, "TOO BAD THERE'S NOTHING LIKE 1–2–3": Jim Seymour, "The Best of Both Worlds," *PC Magazine*, November 24, 1987 (vol. 6, no. 20), p. 103.

Page 40, "THAT'S NOT BECAUSE MAC'S CUTE": J. Seymour, "Ease of Use Brings Other 90 Percent of Market into Microcomputing," *PC Week*, May 8, 1984 (vol. 1, no. 18), p. 19.

Page 40, "I HAVE NEVER LIKED MICE, EXCEPT FOR MICKEY": George Vinall, "Mice Are Nice Ideas, But of Dubious Value for Business Users," *PC Week*, April 24, 1984 (vol. 1, no. 16), p. 21

Page 40, "THEY DON'T USE THOSE CUTE LITTLE ICONS": Stan Miaskowski, "Looking Beyond the DOS Prompt," *Byte IBM Special Edition* (Fall 1989): 107.

Page 40, "WHO WANTS CUTE?": Robert Nichols, "Who Wants Cute?" *InfoWorld*, March 26, 1984, p. 8.

Page 40, "A MAN'S COMPUTER DESIGNED BY *MEN* FOR MEN": Cited in Steven Levy, *Insanely Great: The Life and Times of the Macintosh, the Computer That Changed Everything* (New York: Viking Penguin, 1994), p. 197.

Page 40, FORD "HAD NO USE FOR BEAUTY ON A MACHINE": Cited in David Gartman, "Harley Earl and the Art and Color Section: The Birth of Styling at General Motors," in *Design History: An Anthology*, ed. Dennis P. Doordan (Cambridge, Mass.: MIT Press, 1995), p. 129.

Page 40, APPLE EXECUTIVE GUY KAWASAKI COMPLAINED: Renee Mathews, "The Mac World According to Kawasaki," *MacWeek*, August 2, 1988 (vol. 2, no. 31), p. 36.

Page 40, "THE USERS OF THOSE BUSINESS MACS": Jim Seymour, "The best of both worlds," *PC Magazine*, November 24, 1987 (vol. 6, no. 20), p. 103.

Page 41, "OF COURSE THERE ARE MANY TECHNICALLY SOPHISTICATED PEOPLE": Robert Nichols, "Who Wants Cute?" *InfoWorld*, March 26, 1984, p. 8.

Page 41, "HEATERS, AIR CONDITIONING, AND AUTOMATIC TRANSMISSIONS": James J. Flink, *The Automobile Age* (Cambridge, Mass.: MIT Press, 1988), p. 163.

Page 41, HIS STYLISTS WERE THE "PRETTY-PICTURE BOYS": Ibid., p. 122.

Page 42, "WITH WINDOWS 3.0'S SUCCESS, MICROSOFT CORP. NOW DOMINATES": Alan Brody, "A New World Order with Microsoft at the Helm; with Windows 3.0's Success, Microsoft Corp. Now Dominates . . . " *Marketing Computers*.

Chapter 3: The Aesthetics of Computer Science

Page 46, "USEFUL BECAUSE OF ITS ELEGANT SIMPLICITY": Stan Miaskowski, "Looking Beyond the DOS Prompt," *Byte IBM Special Edition* (Fall 1989): 110.

Page 46, WRITES THE ASTRONOMER, AUTHOR, AND COMPUTER EXPERT CLIFFORD STOLL: Clifford Stoll, *Silicon Snake Oil* (New York: Doubleday, 1995), pp. 71–72.

Page 47, "'FEATURITIS,'" TED NELSON WRITES: Theodor Holm Nelson, "The Right Way to Think About Software Design," in *The Art of Human-Computer Interface Design*, ed. Brenda Laurel (Reading, Mass.: Addison-Wesley, 1990), p. 236.

Page 47, "THE UNIFIED APPEARANCE WE WERE LOOKING FOR": James J. Flink, *The Automobile Age* (Cambridge, Mass.: MIT Press, 1988), p. 236.

Page 47, "UNIFICATION OF FORMERLY UNCOORDINATED ELEMENTS": Ibid., p. 237.

Page 48, "WERE THESE USELESS FEATURES SIMPLY ADD-ON WHISTLES": Clifford Stoll, *Silicon Snake Oil* (New York: Doubleday, 1995), p. 72.

Page 48, "MICROSOFT NEEDS A THOUSAND PAGES": Ibid., p. 66.

Chapter 4: Rise of the Desktop

Page 67, THE PRESIDENT OF DIGITAL EQUIPMENT CORPORATION . . . ANNOUNCED THAT: Cited in Clifford Stoll, *Silicon Snake Oil* (New York: Doubleday, 1995), p. 12.

Page 70, THEY HOPED THAT USERS WOULD JUDGE: D. M. Ritchie and K. Thompson, "The UNIX Time-Sharing System," *Bell System Technical Journal*, July–August 1978 (vol. 57, no. 6, part 2), p. 1906.

Page 74, "IBM KNOWS VERY WELL IT CAN'T SELL OR RENT

A COMPUTER TO ME": Cited in Marc H. Miller, *Something for Everyone: The 1964–65 New York World's Fair* (New York: Flushing Council on Culture and the Arts, 1995), p.33.

Page 77, "ALL OF US THOUGHT THE ALTO DISPLAY WAS INCREDIBLY SMALL": Tekla S. Perry and Paul Wallich, "Inside the PARC: The 'Information Architects,'" *IEEE* [Institute of Electrical and Electronics Engineering] *Spectrum*, October 1985, p. 71.

Page 79, "I THOUGHT CURSOR KEYS WERE MUCH BETTER": Ibid., p. 69.

Page 79, "WE WERE SURPRISED TIME AND AGAIN," SAYS BOB TAYLOR: Howard Rheingold, *Tools for Thought: The People and Ideas Behind the Next Computer Revolution* (New York: Computer Book Division/Simon & Schuster, 1985), p. 212.

Page 80, "CAN'T ACT. CAN'T SING. BALDING": Arlene Croce, *The Fred Astaire and Ginger Rogers Book* (New York: Vintage Books, 1977), p. 14.

Page 80, FOR XEROX TO BECOME "THE ARCHITECT OF INFORMATION": Howard Rheingold, *Tools for Thought: The People and Ideas Behind the Next Computer Revolution* (New York: Computer Book Division/Simon & Schuster, 1985), p. 208.

Page 81, FELLOW TECHNOLOGISTS REGARDED HIS "VIRTUOSO DESIGN": Steven Levy, *Insanely Great: The Life and Times of the Macintosh, the Computer That Changed Everything* (New York: Viking Penguin, 1994), p. 81.

Page 82, "IF YOU MISTYPED A SINGLE CHARACTER OF THE FILE (AS I OFTEN DID)": Ibid., p. 99.

Page 83, "TOO SLOW, HAVING LITTLE SOFTWARE. . . ": Andrew Pollack, "For Apple, rebound and new computer," *New York Times*, September 15, 1986, sec. D, p. 1.

Page 84, BILL GATES WRITES: Bill Gates, with Nathan Myhrvold and Peter Rinearson, *The Road Ahead* (New York: Viking, 1995), pp. 51–52.

Page 84, TO PRONOUNCE IT "RATHER IMPRESSIVE": Gregg Williams, "The Apple Macintosh Computer," *Byte* (February 1984): 53.

Page 84, "I HATE THE MOUSE. I HATE THE ICONS": Rick Vizachero, "Mac Believers Shout Icon, but My Reaction Is I Can't," *Government Computer News*, Jan. 8, 1988 (vol. 7, no. 1), p. 40.

Page 84, "THE MACINTOSH'S OPERATING SYSTEM IS FRIENDLY": Mark S. Jennings, "Evaluating the Macintosh Finder," *Byte* (December 1984): A101.

Page 84, "USERS ARE NOVICES ONLY ONCE": Ibid., p. A94.

Page 84, "THE JURY IS STILL OUT," ACCORDING TO A 1986 ARTICLE: "Personal Computers Part 2: Applications–Lessons Learned," *IEEE* [Institute of Electrical and Electronics Engineering] *Spectrum* (May 1986): 63.

Page 85, "THE JURY IS STILL DEFINITELY OUT" SAID A 1989 ARTICLE: Stan Miaskowski, "Looking Beyond the DOS Prompt," *Byte IBM Special Edition* (Fall 1989): 107.

Page 85, "STILL-DEEP-SEATED AVERSION TO MOUSE USE": Ibid., p. 107.

Page 85, ENGELBART BELIEVED THAT THE DISCOVERIES OF HIS "AUGMENTATION RESEARCH CENTER": Howard Rheingold, *Tools for Thought: The People and Ideas Behind the Next Computer Revolution* (New York: Computer Book Division/Simon & Schuster, 1985), p. 197.

Chapter 5: Beyond the Desktop

Page 87, "LIKE MANY OTHER BRILLIANT IDEAS": Steven Levy, *Insanely Great: The Life and Times of the Macintosh, the Computer That Changed Everything* (New York: Viking Penguin, 1994), p. 70.

Page 89, KAY HIMSELF REFERS TO EXACTLY THIS ISSUE: Alan Kay, "User Interface, a Personal View," in *The Art of Human-Computer Interface Design*, ed. Brenda Laurel (Reading, Mass.: Addison-Wesley, 1990), p. 200.

Page 100, *OTHER* PEOPLE MAKE THIS CLAIM: For example, Linda uses "an extremely powerful, but simple, primitive to